THE ELEMENTS OF THE TAROT

A.T. Mann has practised astrology and tarot professionally for more than twenty years and has written many books on these and other subjects. He teaches at a school for astrology and psychology in Copenhagen, and practises as an architectural and graphic designer.

D1304374

The *Elements Of* is a series designed to present high quality introductions to a broad range of essential subjects.

The books are commissioned specifically from experts in their fields. They provide readable and often unique views of the various topics covered, and are therefore of interest both to those who have some knowledge of the subject, as well as those who are approaching it for the first time.

Many of these concise yet comprehensive books have practical suggestions and exercises which allow personal experience as well as theoretical understanding, and offer a valuable source of information on many important themes.

In the same series

THE ELEMENTS OF
THE TAROT

A T Mann

THE MAGICIAN.

ELEMENT

Shaftesbury, Dorset • Rockport, Massachusetts
Brisbane, Queensland

First published in Great Britain in 1993 by
Element Books Limited
Shaftesbury, Dorset SP7 8BP

Published in the USA in 1993 by
Element Books, Inc.
PO Box 830, Rockport, MA 01966

Published in Australia in 1993 by
Element Books Limited for
Jacaranda Wiley Limited
33 Park Road, Milton, Brisbane 4064

Reprinted 1994
Reprinted February and June 1995

Cover illustration from the Rider Waite Tarot
Cover design by Max Fairbrother
Typeset by the Electronic Book Factory Ltd, Fife, Scotland
Printed and bound in Great Britain by
Biddles Ltd, Guildford and King's Lynn

British Library Cataloguing in Publication
Data available

Library of Congress Cataloging in Publication
Data available

ISBN 1–85230–422–7

THE MAGICIAN.

CONTENTS

ACKNOWLEDGEMENTS

I would like to thank my friend and associate Derek Seagrief for reading parts of the text and for his penetrating and perceptive comments. I thank Michael Mann for suggesting the book and Julia McCutchen for her help in editing the text. And I thank my wife Lise-Lotte for her helpful comments and support throughout the process of writing this book.

THE MAGICIAN

PREFACE

My first introduction to the tarot was a reading in San Francisco in 1968 which proved to be an inner and outer map for the next four years of my life. The accuracy of the reading was astounding and the support this process gave me was inestimable. When I returned from an extended Journey to the East in 1972, I taught myself astrology and tarot together by designing and painting an astrological tarot deck, which I have used ever since. These two have remained inseparable disciplines for me ever since. Astrology has taught me about time and its cycles, while the tarot has always enabled me to look inside for the questions and answers. With this book I go back to the roots of traditional tarot with a new perspective and with the hope that other students such as myself will learn to use the tarot as a guide to the path of the soul.

Tad Mann
Copenhagen 1993

THE MAGICIAN.

1 · WHAT IS THE TAROT?

Tarot is one of the most important forms of western mysticism and has exerted its magical influence for over six hundred years. The cards seem antique and lyrical but carry a symbolism which has stimulated and attracted many searchers after the truth.

Historically the tarot is seen as a mantic art, a form of divination, a way for knowing about the future, a device for telling fortunes. However, the traditions from which the tarot emerged and the interest it has aroused in aware and enlightened people signal its higher functions. The use and understanding of the ancient and mystical art of the tarot cards is a way to develop a recognition of the existence of hidden knowledge within the psyche and awakens deeper layers of soul experience.

While the legends say that the cards are an ancient Egyptian hieroglyphic book of seventy-eight tablets, or engraved plates from Chaldean mystery religions, their inner meaning is indeed a book of philosophy, psychology and spirituality. The tarot cards are symbolic keys whose function is to open up the psyche to new ideas, concepts, feelings and spiritual possibilities. Tarot symbols both conceal and reveal their mysteries according to our ability to concentrate or meditate upon them. The deeper we can go into their world, the more they will awaken true contact with the soul.

The tarot is a book with many sources, being a summation

1

of the Western Mystery Tradition. Tarot contains elements of astrology, cabbala, numerology, alchemy, magic, mythology, Egyptology, religion, Christian mysticism, Eastern philosophy, psychology and metaphysics and yet its form makes it available to everyone, whatever their level of understanding. In this sense it is unique.

HOW DOES THE TAROT FUNCTION?

The oldest beliefs about the tarot can be described by the term *cartomancy*, which is divination by cards. It was believed that mysterious Fate guides the shuffling and selection of cards. Each moment has a unique and magical quality which is divined by and reflected in the cards, just as it may also be seen by reading tea leaves, clouds in the sky, bones, the entrails of animals, stones, seeds or dice. The random shuffling mixes the vocabulary of symbols contained within the cards into a chaotic jumble, and the act of laying the cards out creates order from that primal chaos. At any moment the cards which are drawn reflect the qualities of the time, just as the seemingly irrelevant images of a dream may be seen to identify particular issues emerging from the unconscious self.

If the cards and their actions are the outer form of the mystery of tarot, the inner secret is about how and why they have such a profound effect upon us. Their operation in the realm of the psyche is becoming more important although the use of tarot for divination is not diminishing in favour of its use as a tool for personal transformation.

Tarot demonstrates that the inner psyche not only has a profound relationship with outer events but provides a symbolic mirror for them. The tarot reading produces certain combinations of symbols which reflect the state of the psyche of the querent (questioner) at a given moment, and provides the inner and outer guidance required to understand a current situation or for initiating the next stage of the process.

This seems an absurd idea, but in recent decades it is a concept which has gained acceptance in the domain of physics and psychology. The objective external viewpoint valued by modern science has been proven to be a fantasy, a logical impossibility. Physicists have realized, despite their initial resistance, that the mere fact that they observe events in the physical world has an effect upon those events. This implies that it is essential to recognize the influence of an observer on the experiment, or that being conscious and present has an effect on the outcome of your life. The truth of this concept was proven in experiments in the micro-world of particle physics, where the illumination and measurement of subatomic collisions affects the outcome of the experiment. If the experiment is unobserved, it would not occur in the same way. This is also true in life. Learning to observe yourself experiencing your life will affect you in profound ways.

Thus the subjective state of a querent has an effect upon the results of the shuffling and layout of the cards, just as in modern physics the expectations of the physicist are known to have an effect upon the results of the experiment. Our state of mind is a primary factor in our present and future unfolding.

Tarot is an ideal process through which to observe, interpret and interact with the operations of the psyche. The images of the cards only reflect what is happening inside, and the way you understand these images parallels the way in which you understand and act in your life. Tarot is a near-perfect mirror of your being.

THE MAGICIAN

2 · THE ORIGINS AND HISTORY OF THE TAROT

It is known that decks of numbered pictorial cards tied together with cords existed in India, China and other far eastern countries and were brought back by members of the Knights Templar during and after the crusades in the holy land, but the crusades ended in the last years of the thirteenth century, more than one hundred years before the appearance of the first tarot decks in Europe. Whether these eastern decks were the inspiration for tarot is not known.

The first tarot decks appeared in medieval Europe in the fifteenth century. The exact date or inventor of the cards is unknown, and there are many candidates for the first deck of tarot cards. It is known that playing card decks with four suits (spade, bastoni, coppe and denari, the forerunners of our suits of spades, clubs, hearts and diamonds), and portraying kings, queens and knights, were used more than a century earlier, and therefore the myth that tarot preceded playing cards is probably exactly that. Tarot decks are unique because they have twenty-two picture cards known as *major trumps* or *major arcana*, used together with a *minor arcana* of fifty-six cards similar to traditional playing cards plus the addition of four extra face cards, making a deck of seventy-eight cards. The word *arcana* means secret or mysterious in Latin, while *trump* is derived from the Latin *trionfi*, which referred to a circular triumphal procession in Roman times but now implies superiority.

The earliest tarots are decorated with medieval images and symbols, and have names such as the Empress, Pope, Emperor, High Priestess, Fool, Magician and Hanged Man, all members of medieval society. In most tarot decks these major cards are numbered from one to twenty-one, with the Fool either zero or left unnumbered. The names and sequence of the cards is by no means standard, as many variations exist.

Many derivations have been suggested for the name *tarot*. It may come from the Latin word *rota* (wheel) which is an anagram of tarot, is used in some decks on the card of the Wheel of Fortune (see Figure 1), and was a magical formula utilized by the Brotherhood of the Rosy Cross. The Egyptian word *Ta-rosh* means 'the royal way,' and similarly it is suggested that tarot is derived from the name of the god of writing and magic, Thoth. Some commentators who accept its Hebrew origin see it as a corruption of the *torah*, the book of the law. On the most exoteric level, *tar* is the Gypsy word for a deck of cards.

The early decks were individually hand-painted and later were block-printed and hand coloured until the popularization of the printing press centuries later.

The **Visconti-Sforza** *tarocchi* cards are one of the earliest known decks, painted in the mid-1400s for the Duke of Milan. They are now in museum collections in New York and Italy. This hand-painted deck contains twenty-two large cards with gold leaf and luxurious finish.

Francois Fibbia, the Prince of Pisa in exile, invented a deck of tarot cards very similar to those known today, composed of forty numbered cards and twenty-two arcana cards. As he died in 1415, this dates his deck as among the earliest.

The **Mantegna** deck, while not identified with the famous painter of the same name, is a beautiful and unusual deck of tarot cards, numbered from one to fifty, divided into five classes of ten cards each. The deck is an image of the universal order as perceived at the time, and portrays a sequence of evolutionary stages from the Prima Causa (Creation) to the

Figure 1   The Wheel of Fortune

Beggar (corresponding to the Fool in modern decks). In Series A are the spheres of creation and the sun, moon and planets; Series B and C contain thirteen of the liberal arts such as grammar, geometry, philosophy, astrology, theology and cosmology; Series D contains Apollo and the nine muses; while Series E is similar to traditional tarot in including images of the pope, the emperor, the king, the doge, the knight, gentleman, a merchant, artisan, valet and beggar. These cards exist in the British Museum and are dated from 1470 to 1485.

Subsequent *tarocchi* (in French, *tarot*) decks numbered seventy-eight cards. In addition to the major arcana are fifty-six minor arcana cards, including sixteen court cards in four suits (pentacles, swords, cups and wands) and named the King and Queen, Knight and Page (or Prince and Princess) and forty minor arcana cards numbered from ace to ten of each suit. These last cards are identical to modern playing cards.

The **Marseilles** deck appeared towards the end of the fifteenth century, using similar subjects but different designs, and retaining the use of the four suits. In the Marseilles deck the Fool is unnumbered and the other major arcana cards have roman numerals. This deck has remained one of the most colourful and popular ever since.

It is assumed by many that tarot cards are of much more ancient origin than the earliest decks. The eighteenth century scholar Court de Gebelin (1725–84) claimed that the major arcana were symbolic of the stages of the Egyptian or Chaldean mysteries. He proposed that the twenty-two major arcana cards were remnants of the book of Thoth, the Egyptian god of writing. He believed that tarot described the creation of the world, organized by the number seven. His deck was seventy-eight cards (seventy-seven plus the Fool); the four suits contained twice seven cards (ten pips plus four court cards), and the major arcana contained thrice seven cards plus the Fool as zero. The designs which accompanied his book in 1781 are the foundation upon which later traditional decks were designed.

The nineteenth century philosopher and cabbalist **Eliphas Levi** identified the source of tarot wisdom and symbolism as the sacred Enochian alphabet of the Hebrews, which had previously been recorded on tablets of gold and ivory, decorated with precious stones and gilt. He believed that even when the tarot did not predict, it revealed something hidden to the wise. Since the Hebrew alphabet has twenty-two letters and its associated tree of life twenty-two paths between the ten Sephiroth, he announced their absolute equivalence (see p. 16). His pronouncements are taken quite literally even today, although there is little evidence for his claims.

A French scholar Gerard Encausse (1865–1917), whose magical name in the Rosicrucian and masonic orders was **Papus,** carried the attributions of Levi further by showing that the entire wisdom transmitted in the tarot was central to the Egyptian mystery religion and that its function was as an initiation device. He also introduced Hebrew number symbolism, called *gematria*, into the tarot in the numbering and numerical value of the cards.

A scholar who transformed the use and study of tarot in modern times was Dr Arthur Edward Waite (1857–1942), a member of the mystical Order of the Golden Dawn, who explored the symbolism of the tarot in his book *The Key to the Tarot*. He also designed a deck which was executed by the artist Pamela Coleman Smith, afterwards called the **Rider Waite** deck, which is the deck we will use as the basis for this book. Waite developed the magical and symbolic aspects of the major arcana cards, introducing many hermetic and rosicrucian images to the cards, and also created images for all of the minor arcana. Previously, all decks had portrayed the minor arcana cards like playing card pips, thus the eight of swords had been a design of eight swords on a card. Waite, however, shows this card as a young woman tied up and blindfolded, surrounded by eight swords plunged into the ground, in front of a hill town fortress. His major structural modification was to change the position of the unnumbered Fool from between arcana XXI and XXII, to identify it with the first letter aleph and the number zero, and to place it before The Magician. Because Waite was aware of the astrological attributions of the cards, he exchanged the positions of Strength (previously XI) and Justice (previously VIII), probably because they are associated with the zodiac signs Leo and Libra.

According to Waite,

> The Tarot embodies symbolical presentations of universal ideas behind which lie all the implicits of the human mind, and it is in this sense that they contain a secret doctrine, which is the realization by the few of truths embedded in the consciousness of all, though they have not passed into express recognition by ordinary men.

Kaplan, *The Classical Tarot*, p. 62.

Waite intended to transmit what were formerly hidden teachings through his deck, and told symbolical stories through the cards in images available to anyone who chose to delve into them. His descriptions of the cards are sometimes vague and evasive, typical of the time when the mystery schools were first presenting their esoteric ideas to the public. But, he was one of the first to do so, and his deck is valued for this.

One of the most controversial magicians of our century was Aleister Crowley, who after a lifetime of study and practice, designed the **Thoth** deck with the artist Lady Freida Harris in the 1940s (see Figure 2). It is the most symbolic and colourful deck ever produced, and it contains Egyptian, Eastern, Greek, medieval and Christian symbolism, and in its structure synthesized the traditions of numerology, alchemy, cabbala and astrology. Crowley was a student of cabbala and tarot, as well as being an initiate of the Order of the Golden Dawn, and he made some fundamental changes in the attributions of the major arcana. He acknowledged the switch in order of

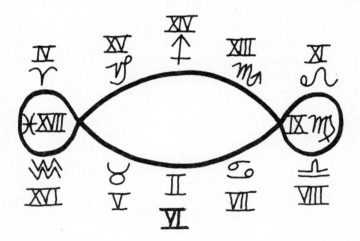

Figure 2   The Double Loop (after Aleister Crowley). Crowley switched the previous attributions of Strength (XI) and Justice (VIII) which spiral around The Hermit (IX), and invented this Double Loop to explain why he also reversed the numbers of The Emperor (IV) and The Star (XVII) around The Moon (XVIII).

9

the trumps VIII (Adjustment = Libra) and XI (Lust = Leo), and also proposed that the trumps IV (The Emperor) and XVII (The Star) should exchange places. Crowley saw the tarot as a magical encyclopedia and as a key to the mysteries which could be utilized by a magician in order to invoke their various energies. They were to him a form of archetypal intelligence which could be incorporated within the psyche and he suggested that one imagine them as living beings, an antidote to the pious and serious approach he saw among his contemporaries.

In recent years the tarot has become extremely popular and its permutations have proliferated. Decks which are only loosely tarot decks have been made using as their foundation the symbolic systems of women, the earth mother goddesses, native Americans, Celts, Arthurian knights, and myriad others. Some of these are worthy of exploration, but many have strayed away from the central concept of the tarot and its archetypal language.

THE MAGICIAN.

3 · THE STRUCTURE AND SYMBOLISM OF THE TAROT

The tarot is seen to contain elements of many representative western mystery traditions because its structure is uniquely suited to satisfy all their various requirements. Indeed, it is astonishing how many different philosophical, religious, psychological and magical systems it seems able to reflect. Successive commentators state that the tarot has one particular true meaning, and all the others are secondary, and the many cultures now represented in tarot decks all derive from the same archetypal foundations. It is the structure of the tarot, contained in the number and symbolism of the cards, that makes this possible.

The adaptability of the tarot is characteristic of a system which arises from the archetypal domain. At their core the cards are powerful because they are images upon which a viewer can project aspects of the self. In this sense the cards are archetypal. We can easily see the Wise Old Man, the Eternal Child, the Fool, the Emperor, the Pope, the Hanged Man, the Empress and Death as archetypal images which exist in us at some deeper level of development. It is therefore a supreme tool for making contact with and

11

learning to communicate with the archetypes of the collective unconscious, those mythological themes whose symbolism illustrate human history, and, by extension, all of the parts of ourselves.

The tarot also utilizes a vocabulary of symbols to carry its meaning. Carl Jung, the Swiss psychologist who studied the significance of symbols and mythology in the human psyche, made a distinction between a sign and a symbol. A sign is a conventional image which possesses a definite meaning or significance, like the IBM logo or the Olympic rings. A symbol, however, is the manifestation of an archetypal pattern which has multiple meanings. Thus a cross may mean Christianity, the earth, a hospital, the national flag of Denmark, or the four cardinal directions of the compass, according to the orientation and background of the observer. Symbols have deeper, more profound significance because they activate instinctive parts of us which may have lain dormant for years or lifetimes, and often carry many layers of meaning simultaneously. They thus contain a power not activated by signs, the function of which is to limit and define meaning.

At the most basic level, tarot is a universal structure expressing a vocabulary of archetypal symbols. Understanding the structure and the symbols and their meaning will allow one to decode any tarot deck, and indeed any archetypal images found in our lives.

NUMBER SYMBOLISM

The primary structural device in tarot is number. Each major arcana card not only has a numerical value but also a Roman numeral which places it in sequence. The numbers and numerals describe their relationship with each other and the whole. Each suit of the minor arcana is numbered from the ace (one) to ten.

Numbers represent actual potencies in nature, such as the sequence of chemical elements in the periodic table, the notes in the musical scale or the wave lengths of colours in the visible spectrum. But, the sequence of natural numbers is more than just a way of counting quantity – it also describes a process which comes into being through time. It is this latter mechanism which tarot uses in its organization. The cards describe a sequence of stages of an archetypal psychological development in which we all participate.

The natural numbers have important symbolic meanings:

Zero   is non-being, the opposite of unity, the latent potential of creativity, the non-manifest and the state of death during which life is transformed. It can be symbolized by blackness, holes, empty space, the underworld and the world egg enwrapped by a snake.

One   is the point, the centre, the focus of creativity, pure spirit, unity and the reduction of all other numbers (all numbers can be divided by one). It can be symbolized by a point or a circle or a sphere, a single centralized object or the Hebrew letter aleph.

Two   is the line, duality, the periphery, an echo, reflection, the shadow and represents the quality of the attraction of opposites which is contained in all processes. It is symbolized by the full or new moon, heaven and earth, black and white squares, pairs of columns, shadows, twins, the yin yang, the mountain, and symmetry around an axis as above-below or right-left.

Three   is the plane, balance and resolution, synthesis and creation, heaven, the action of unity upon duality. It is symbolized by the triangle, the three dimensions, the trinity.

Four   is the solid, manifest world, earth, the physical domain and the quaternity of integration as the four elements or the four psychological types. It is symbolized by the cross, square and cube, the four cardinal points, four fixed zodiac signs and the beasts of the Apocalypse or Ezekiel.

Five   is man, time, the quintessence of being, the centre of the manifest universe. It is symbolized by the pentagram and pentagon, and the square or cube with a central point, the star, the human body, the golden section mathematical proportion derived from the pentagon which governs the pattern of growth in same plants.

Six is equilibrium, the human soul, self consciousness capable of experience, the six directions of space, trial and effort. It is symbolized by the Seal of Solomon or the Star of David, an upward and downward pointing triangle of the elements intersecting, and the elemental plane.

Seven is perfect order, bliss, the essence of being, the completion of a cycle or period, the chakras, the planetary spheres and their gods and goddesses. It is symbolized by the seven planets, the constellation of the Great Bear, the rainbow colours, the chakra lotuses, the musical scale, the Seal of Solomon with a point of spirit in the centre.

Eight is thought and intellection, the doubled quaternity, the resurrection, the enclosure, the eight cardinal and intermediate directions, the firmament or realm of the fixed stars. It is symbolized by the eight-pointed star, the double square or double cube, the caduceus, and the infinity symbol.

Nine is the tripled trinity, being, pleasure, truth, the mystic number, integration of physical, intellectual and spiritual worlds. It is symbolized by three intersecting triangles.

Ten is the return to unity, spiritual achievement, the totality of the universe, and perfection. It is symbolized by two intersecting pentacles.

Eleven is transition, excess and conflict, duality incapable of resolution.

Twelve is cosmic order and salvation, the astrological language, the year, the wheel of becoming. It is symbolized by the zodiac or rings of flowers.

Each card carries its quality as number in addition to its other symbolism, and also its significance as a particular stage of a process. Many of the cards, and particularly the major arcana cards, also contain references to the other numbers in shapes, patterns, objects which have certain symmetries or quantities, and in many other ways, even when the visible number implies hidden numbers. For example, it is significant that the belt worn by the Fool has seven small discs, corresponding to the visible spectrum or the seven ancient planets, attributes of the 'real' world. The five discs hidden behind him complete the zodiacal number twelve and show that youthful energy is subject to fate and that its true humanity is still hidden.

THE FOUR ELEMENTS

When tarot first appeared the primary philosophical device for organizing the world was the four elements. Plato spoke of the world being composed of the elements fire, earth, air and water. Everything in the world, including human beings, are made of varying proportions of these four elements. In various cultures these four elements correspond to:

- The elements from which god created the universe.
- The four classes of medieval society: nobility, clergy, merchants and peasants
- The four magical weapons: the wand, pentacle, sword and cup.
- The four cardinal directions: east, south, west and north.
- Jung's four psychological types: intuition, sensation, thinking and feeling.
- The four substances in alchemy: mercury, salt, sulphur and water.
- The four letters of the divine name of god in Hebrew, the Tetragrammaton: *yod, heh, vau, heh.*
- The four worlds or planes of existence of the cabbalists: the archetypal world, the world of creation, the world of formation, and the world of action.
- The four classes of magical spirits: sylphs, gnomes, watersprites and elves.
- The four beasts of the Apocalypse or the vision of Ezekiel: lion, bull, man and eagle.

The minor arcana of tarot is divided into four suits – wands, pentacles, swords and cups. The sequence of ten numbers and four court cards within each suit describes a process of development, both physical, psychological and spiritual from first inspiration to final manifestation.

CABBALA, ASTROLOGY AND THE SEQUENCE OF THE CARDS

The sequence of the major arcana cards is a contentious issue about which few commentators agree. In many early decks the number sequence changes from deck to deck, and indeed was rarely included in the designs of the cards.

Tarot adepts in the late nineteenth and early twentieth centuries identified the cards with the sequence of twenty-two Hebrew letters which are the foundation of the Jewish mystical cabbala because they are symbols which describe all reality, rather than just signs as they are in our languages.

The twenty-two Hebrew letters are organized into three types: three mother letters corresponding to the elements fire, air and water; seven single letters corresponding to planets; and twelve double letters corresponding to zodiac signs. The entire major arcana itself is the fourth element earth. Because the major arcana sequence seemed to follow the sequence of the letters and they had the same number of components, the correspondence between the two was natural.

The tree of life is a blueprint of perfect manifestation in the universe showing the unfolding transition from God at the top to Man at the bottom, and allows many layers of interpretation, including into three vertical pillars, seven horizontal hierarchies, and so on. In Figure 3 the ten sephira, which are emanations of the divine and correspond in tarot to the numbered minor arcana cards, are connected by twenty-two paths or channels of divine influence, which correspond to the major arcana cards. The combination of ten numbers and twenty-two letters allows the tree to function as a magical alphabet corresponding to the entire world. This important key was used to organize the sequence of the cards.

Eliphas Levi and Papus both placed the unnumbered Fool between arcana XX, Judgment and XXI, The World. Waite later changed the numerology and correspondences of the

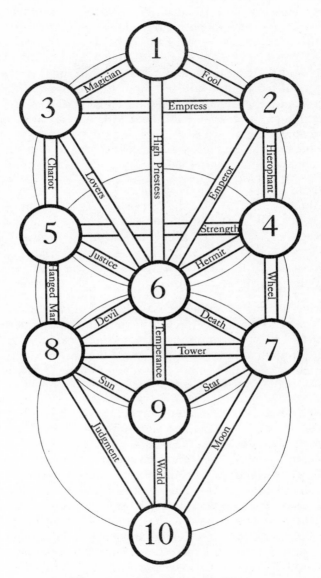

Figure 3   The Tree of Life

entire sequence by placing the Fool before the Magician as zero. This was wise because it is not only more logical from a mathematical viewpoint, but also brings a greater power to the correlations, because the Hebrew letter aleph signifies 'the beginning'. In Waite's new sequence the Fool, the Hanged Man and the Last Judgment correspond to the three 'mother' letters of the Hebrew alphabet and the elements: the Fool is aleph and the element air; the Hanged Man is mem and the element water; and the Last Judgment is shin and the element fire.

The correlations of planets to the major arcana single letters are:

Beth	I	The Magician	Mercury
Gimel	II	The High Priestess	Moon
Daleth	III	The Empress	Venus
Kaph	X	The Wheel of Fortune	Jupiter
Peh	XVI	The Tower	Mars
Resh	XVIII	The Sun	Sun
Tau	XXI	The World	Saturn

The correlation of zodiac signs with major arcana was changed by Waite, so that the cards VIII, Justice and XI, Strength in the Levi and Papus attributions became transposed. He reasoned that Strength is more appropriate for the zodiac sign Leo and Justice is a classic symbol for the sign Libra, with which we agree. Waite's changes create the following sequence:

Heh	IV	The Emperor	Aries
Vau	V	The Hierophant	Taurus
Zain	VI	The Lovers	Gemini
Cheth	VII	The Chariot	Cancer
Teth	VIII	Strength	Leo
Yod	IX	The Hermit	Virgo
Lamed	XI	Justice	Libra
Nun	XIII	Death	Scorpio
Samech	XIV	Temperance	Sagittarius
Ayin	XV	Devil	Capricorn
Tzaddi	XVII	The Star	Aquarius
Qoph	XVIII	The Moon	Pisces

The final sequence of Waite is as follows:

0	The Fool	Air (and Uranus)
I	The Magician	Mercury
II	The High Priestess	Moon
III	The Empress	Venus
IV	The Emperor	Aries
V	The Hierophant	Taurus
VI	The Lovers	Gemini
VII	The Chariot	Cancer
VIII	Strength	Leo
IX	The Hermit	Virgo
X	The Wheel of Fortune	Jupiter
XI	Justice	Libra
XII	The Hanged Man	Water (and Neptune)
XIII	Death	Scorpio
XIV	Temperance	Sagittarius
XV	The Devil	Capricorn
XVI	The Tower	Mars
XVII	The Star	Aquarius
XVIII	The Moon	Pisces
XIX	The Sun	Sun
XX	The Last Judgment	Fire (and Pluto)
XXI	The World	Saturn

ASTROLOGY AND THE CARDS

The attributions of the major arcana with the elements and astrological signs and planets is accepted as a primary structure of the tarot, although there are many arrangements for merging the two disciplines. The correlation is particularly valuable because astrology defines very clear personality types and physical and psychological actions to individual signs, planets and aspects between planets which can be used to further enrich the tarot symbolism, although a valid criticism of this is that the images of tarot deserve to remain associations of the unconscious, rather than as a rational system like astrology.

Apart from the structure of tarot, astrological symbols abound in the tarot. Images such as the lion in the Strength card obviously correlate with the sign Leo; the Chariot with lunar crescents outside the walls of a city evokes the sign Cancer; similarly the lunar images of the High Priestess mark her as a goddess of the moon; the association of the Death card with the sign Scorpio is clear; the garden couch of the Empress is decorated with a venus symbol upon a heart, clearly evoking Venus; the Tower is destroyed by a burst of energy which is obviously of the planet Mars; and the Sun card literally corresponds to the astrological symbolism of the sun. The symbols bring an ancient and archetypal quality to the cards which evoke deep feelings within us.

Astrology is used to organize and interpret the court cards and minor arcana cards, in addition to its use in the major arcana.

TAROT SYMBOLISM

The tarot cards use a language of symbols which refer to psychological processes as well as external events in life, as Jung discovered. In order to use the cards it is important to understand some of the more common symbols. These symbols are archetypal in that they key off deep memories or activate contents within our collective unconscious which are not always available to our conscious minds. The language is similar to that of dream interpretation.

Symbols fall into many categories and are derived from architecture, particularly because visualizing buildings was seen as a structure for improving the memory in medieval times, and the art of memory had a 'square art' which utilized such symbols. Many symbols are natural plants, animals or objects in the world, while others are derived from human endeavour and crafted objects.

Pairs of columns appear in a number of the cards quite naturally, because they are figures of authority such as the High Priestess, the Hierophant and Justice. They symbolize the physical world and its vested authorities. The Greek

Iamblichus was initiated into the Egyptian mysteries and saw a temple with twenty-two pairs of columns, between each of which were frescos depicting mystical figures and symbols facing each other in pairs. Each picture represented a stage of the initiation process and is reproduced in the tarot cards. The columns in some of the cards may be symbolic of this mystery temple. Such column pairs are also gateways from one place to another, but, more importantly, from one state of mind or attitude to another. These cards therefore symbolize transition and permanent change of values. When there are black and white columns, such as in the High Priestess, they additionally show dualities such as male/female, conscious/unconscious, right/left, etc. Where the columns are abstracted, such as in the card of the Chariot, they signify taking on authority oneself.

Stars and **canopies** symbolize the higher world available through increased awareness. Stars symbolize the astrological qualities which synchronize with our life pattern, and show the higher language of the heavens. They often represent actual zodiac constellations or constellations such as the Pleiades or Sirius which were worshipped by the Egyptians and other cultures. The stars are also bodies encasing the spirit, mind and soul. In esoteric astrology the seven stars of the Great Bear represent the seven solar systems from which the present world was evolved.

The **throne** is dominion, power, strength and fixed being, often associated with royalty. In some of the cards the throne is symbolic of the domain of the archetype, for example in the Empress where the throne is created in nature and indeed is the natural world, or in the Devil where the throne is a black cube of stone to which the female and male natures are chained. Both the throne and cube are symbolic of the physical world itself.

The **pyramid** is the resolution and transfiguration of the physical world symbolized by the four sides on the ground, and the higher, transcendent reality symbolized by the apex or crown.

The **square** and the **triangle** are the plane symbols of the cube and pyramid in three dimensions. The square is the physical world, solidity and persistence, and signifies the human being who is not evolved and has not achieved inner unity. The triangle is the trinity, the resolution of duality by a third, higher integrating influence at its apex, which is often taken to be consciousness. When the triangle points downwards it shows immersion in matter, dominance by the body or physical demands, and the principle of unconsciousness. The Seal of Solomon or Star of David is the integration between lower and higher, or of unconscious and conscious qualities.

The **sphere** symbolizes god, completion and also the cosmos within which all activity takes place. When it is surmounted by a cross, it is the orb of worldly power with spiritual understanding or papal dominance.

Towers symbolize the act of rising above the mundane physical world to higher realms, a means of ascent, and a linking of earth to heaven. The windows shown in a tower may indicate the various levels of being within the human body, with the higher windows representing higher qualities. A lighthouse is high illumination. A pair of towers shows the duality between individual power and life energy.

The **crown** is dominion, royal position and high status. Many believe it to be a physical reflection of the human aura which demonstrates our level of spiritual development in its colours. The triple tiara shows power over the three worlds of the physical, emotional and mental domains.

The **sceptre** is a magic wand, symbolic of the phallus or the thunderbolt as sources of energy and fertility, as well as being linked to the world axis. The sceptre is often abstracted as the fleur-de-lys so often found in decorations on the cards.

Keys are to open the secret doctrine, to unlock the recesses of ourselves.

An **arrow** is the will, spirit or the energy and one-pointedness of the element fire.

Many tarot symbols are animals or plants:

A **snake** symbolizes time, and when forming a circle biting its tail or in the figure-eight shape of the lemniscate is infinity. It signifies the cyclic nature of the world and energy required to power the cycles of life.

Corn is fertility and plenty as a symbol of the Great Mother or grain goddess, as well as of ritual fertilization, death and renewal. The **cornfield** is fertility and a loving environment.

Roses are symbols of love, but also mystical and alchemical correlates with the heart.

Trees are the process of evolution and integration. In ancient times they were sacred spirits and the way by which spirits descended to the world and by which the souls of humanity reached heaven.

Because the **sunflower** moves with the sun it is solar and leonine.

The **dog** is loyalty, instinct and faithfulness, as well as being the guardian of the underworld of the unconscious. **Cats** are the perceptive power and pure consciousness of the feminine.

Eagles and **hawks** are temporal power, dominion and strength. They fly with the sun god and when symbolized with a solar disc are Egyptian deities. The **phoenix** symbolizes rebirth and renewal through destruction.

Butterflies and **bees** are symbolic of the soul, rebirth and eternal life.

Crabs, **lobsters** and other crustaceans emerge, like humanity, from the unconscious sea and represent the fertilizing power of water.

Mountains symbolize the quest, the need to ascend, of meditation and higher realms of the self. Mountains in the distance imply the embarkation upon the journey to wholeness.

Lightning is inspiration and a direct communication with the gods and goddesses, intuition and divine intercession.

Barren landscapes are devoid of love and affection.

THE MAGICIAN.

4 · THE 22 MAJOR ARCANA CARDS

The twenty-two major arcana cards describe the process from the pure state of the unnumbered Fool to the completion of the World.

Each of the cards described in the sequence are presented from a variety of viewpoints which will enhance your understanding of the tarot major arcana, and will illuminate qualities associated with the cards which are often not identified, such as a guided imagery and an affirmation.

Each card will be described, to draw attention to the images, symbols and their interaction in the overall composition of the card. The Symbolism of the card identifies the inner, psychological meaning of the images and actions portrayed in the card, as well as an initiatory lesson to be learned from the card. The Guided Imagery is intended to provide the atmosphere of discovery and inner experience associated with the card. These images are best read to you, or tape-recorded slowly and clearly. The images support and reinforce the deeper meanings of the cards and communicate their core significance to the self.

The Meaning describes the manifestations of the card and its symbolism in life situations, often called the divinatory meaning of the cards. In many books on the tarot there are also meanings used when the card is upside down or reversed, which are often considered more difficult and describe negative qualities associated with the cards. Occasionally the negative meanings bear little relationship to the upright significance of the cards. Thus Waite describes the divinatory meaning of the Magician reversed as 'Physician, Magus, mental disease, disgrace, disquiet'. In more recent times it has become an antique practice to designate reversed meanings for the cards. In reality the reversed cards signify shadow qualities, the underlying unconscious motives which are other, sometimes darker, aspects of our being which are yet inseparable from our totality. These shadow qualities simply bring the lighter qualities into sharper focus. The reversed card also signifies the need to penetrate more deeply, to look more vigilantly into and to take more time trying to understand the hidden significance of a certain time or quality. A separate meaning would only exaggerate such splits.

The Affirmation is a useful device for coming into a deeper and more immediate relationship with the qualities embodied in the cards.

It is important to remember that although the major arcana cards depict medieval scenes, the individuals in them and their magical implements, they are also symbols of the collective unconscious, the common psychic inheritance shared by all humanity which lies within everyone. You may even find that you remember these people, places and scenes from other lives or deeper layers of your psyche.

THE FOOL
The Spirit of Aethyr

Arcanum Zero
The planet Uranus and the
element Air
Key Word: Individuation
Hebrew Letter: Aleph א

A questing and confident youth begins his journey standing on a mountain precipice high above the world. He looks up rather than down, despite the dog barking at his heels. He wears beautiful clothes decorated with mystical symbols and a fool's cap with a feather. Suspended from the wand over his shoulder is an embroidered bag containing his worldly possessions. He holds a rose in his left hand and his face is intelligent, blissful and radiant, like the sun at his back. He is the pure man, awaiting the experiences of the world which will fulfil his expectations and dreams.

The Symbolic Fool
The Fool is the eternal child beginning the journey to enlightenment, symbolized by his ambiguous number zero and his daring descent from the top of the mountain. He is the element Air representing the spontaneous mind which contains our fantasies, projections, thoughts and understanding,

but which is uncontrolled and prone to erratic and unpredictable behaviour, characteristic of the planet Uranus. His zodiacal belt symbolizes his journey to individuation through the planetary spheres. He carries all the elements except the sword of discrimination (see p.74) – he believes too readily and can easily be misled by outer appearances or attractive ideas. He is an empty canvas waiting for a painter who can take risks.

Guided Imagery
'Having effortlessly ascended to the mountain top, you survey the beautiful landscape below the mountain peak upon which you stand. Your shadow, cast by the powerful sun at your back, extends across hill and vale, integrating itself within the marvellous and beautiful landscape below, breaking down into thousands of details, and changing its overall form from moment to moment. As you spontaneously leap across the first precipice towards an unknown destiny in the far distance, you realize that you must descend through that shadow that moves as you do, beyond into the clear light of day.'

The Meaning
Childlike enthusiasm; awakening perceptions of the world; mental spontaneity leading either to folly or wisdom. Beginning an adventure without considering the consequences. An 'all or none' attitude.

Affirmation
'The truth and radiance of my inner child will guide me through unlimited possibilities as I venture out into the unknown world.'

THE MAGICIAN
The Magus of Power

Arcanum One
The planet Mercury
Key Word: Initiation
Hebrew Letter: Beth ב

THE MAGICIAN.

A magically robed youth holds a wand aloft in his right hand, while pointing down to the flower-covered ground with his left, linking the spiritual with the earthly world. He looks down upon the pentacle, cup, sword and wand, his magical implements on the table. Floating above his head is the horizontal figure-of-eight, the lemniscate or infinity sign, showing the attainment of eternal knowledge in life. The columns supporting the table indicate the need to raise consciousness above the world of the senses. The red and white motif of flowers and his robes show that he embodies the synthesis of physical and spiritual worlds.

The Symbolic Magician
The magician is the mind, alternately instinctive and profound, which must be juggled and empowered by our will. He is concentrated without effort, and guided by inner rhythms. The magic of Mercury brings down higher virtue to things

below and allows communication between levels within. The pentacle, cup, sword and wand are his magical implements which symbolize the divine in the four elements expressed through the psychological types – the aspects of the self which must be brought into balance and equilibrium. They lie upon the four-fold table, which is the firmament and foundation of the human endeavour towards synthesis. The double-ended wand, the red and white colours, and his upward and downward pointing gestures all illustrate the duality which the magician within us must conquer with wisdom. The infinity symbol over his head and the snake biting its tail around his waist imply that the ability to find unity through meditation and concentration lies above and around us.

Guided Imagery
'As you walk within the walled garden on a radiant day, a stream symbolizing life energy parts it in two. The bridge joining the halves is higher mind, and the power of the magician within you depends upon knowing both sides. As you cross over, you become aware of the elevated view the bridge affords, making you feel bright and confident of inner ideas. The darkness and insecurity in the recesses of your changeable mind become transformed into the light of conscious wisdom within the self. The transformation happens in a divine instant, bringing together your contradictory parts. You are juggling the pentacle, cup, wand and sword in a masterly way, knowing that they are the tools of your enlightenment. Now you see the light is within yourself.'

The Meaning
Exploration of consciousness leads to wisdom; the search for meaning as a magical action; transforming the basic material of the unaware self. The correct application of willpower depends upon adapting to existing forces, preferring thought over action. Communication skills bring access to the divine.

Affirmation
'I concentrate without effort, pay attention, and transform work into play, thereby communicating magical talents through my clarity of self.'

THE HIGH PRIESTESS
Priestess of the Silver Star

Arcanum Two
The Moon
Key Word: Hidden Knowledge
Hebrew Letter: Gimel ⅃

The High Priestess in early tarot decks is called the Papess, evoking the mythical Pope Joan of the ninth century, and is also Juno, the priestess Diana of the Eleusinian mysteries, or the Celtic triple goddess. She contains the many dimensions of feminine power, expressing the polarity between masculine law and feminine imagination. She wears the blue vestments of Isis – a crown of two horn-shaped crescents astride a lunar orb – and stands on a waxing crescent moon. On her chest is a solar cross and under her robes she carries the scrolls of the Hebrew torah (with the last letter hidden), because in her antiquity she contains pagan, Egyptian, Jewish and Christian authority. Her cubic throne of unadorned and pure matter sits between black and white lotus pillars of the Egyptian mystery temple.

The Symbolic High Priestess
Indigo and silver colours, the horns and orb of Isis, and the arch symbolizing the lunar cycle all belong to the moon

goddess. She symbolizes the image-making and illumination of the feminine energy. Her blue robes are set off against a curtain illustrating the tree of life, showing that her power derives from her position on the central pillar of the tree. She is open and changeable, wise and dark, not judgmental as she is able to identify with both poles of all feelings, shown by the crescent foundation and the black and white columns. She signifies the unpredictable and contrary ways by which the soul expresses its uniting intelligence.

Guided Imagery
'You wander through the forest, further and further away from the city. The flowing stream which accompanies you in the journey snakes around and you find yourself upon a plateau surrounded by the swirling waters. Boarding a moored boat you travel down the stream of consciousness, as you do so being invaded by visions of past and future. The awesome banks on either side are present truths, bounding your journey and defining your path. Although out of control in the dark waters, you bring new insight into the shadows you have always feared within yourself. The torch you carry sheds light on your own unconscious source of wisdom and power. In the heart of darkness you find your own light. You juggled life, but now your knowing arises from within yourself.'

The Meaning
Hidden life truths revealed through intuition, divination, feminine wisdom and revelation. Taking emotional chances; foresight; fluctuation; forces of nature and psychic or artistic abilities. Inspired silence and secrecy; healing magic; walking the path of destiny. Emotional balance derived from foresight: overwhelming enthusiasm.

Affirmation
'In searching my inner darkness I discover the foundation of my outer knowing. My integrity grows from intuition and perception.'

THE EMPRESS
Daughter of the Mighty Ones

Arcanum Three
The planet Venus
Key Word: Nature
Hebrew Letter: Daleth

The beautiful Empress holds a sceptre of physical dominion and sits upon her pillow throne which bears a shield decorated with the symbol of Venus. She sits within her protected domain of ripened corn, cypress trees and rushing water as the goddess of fertility and abundance, and her head crowned with the twelve stars shows her as mistress of the births of all souls. She bestows love and life, and also takes them away. She represents the wilderness of the instincts, which must be subdued and nurtured to promote fruitfulness.

The Symbolic Empress
She is essential fecundity and the joyful love of all living things and the gateway into the world of form, but also contains sorrowful power over the dark mysteries of death. Her red throne denotes pure instinct and her robe is covered with pomegranates of universal integration. Her power emerges from the unconscious and she activates the deep emotional

core of all beings. Her upturned lunar crescent and sheaf of harvested wheat show that maturity requires leaving the protection of the mother, and that sacrifice is required to dominate the instinctual nature.

Guided Imagery
'As you walk through the field of ripe wheat, the golden grain stretches as far as you can see, bounded only by distant mountain ranges. Birds sing, bees buzz and you can smell myriad flowers and hear the growth all around you. Everything is joy and abundance. You approach a towering cypress tree which penetrates the edge of a deep, clear pool of water, its roots rending the dark, rich soil and emerging from the dark water. You feel the presence of a radiant mother-bride near, bestowing her blessings and love on you and fertilizing your actions performed in her honour. As you lie upon the fragrant soil, you feel as though you could stay forever in the protection of the womb of nature and her goddesses.'

The Meaning
The path of harmony through emotional conflict. Fruitfulness and fertility and their relationship to attachment and physical value. Creating life leads to the death of your previous state, and openness to your natural acts can bring closer contacts, but also vulnerability. Try to integrate and harmonize with others.

Affirmation
'I nurture my creative potential as a gateway for my highest personal fulfilment. I give love and support to others to express my feeling of inner peace, and accept their beauty and affection with wisdom.'

THE EMPEROR
Son of the Morning,
Chief Among the Mighty

Arcanum Four
The sign Aries
Key Word: Law
Hebrew Letter: Heh 𝕳

THE EMPEROR.

The crowned Emperor sits on his cubic throne with ram's head carvings holding an ankh sceptre and a globe. He is the lord of thought and action, parent with the Empress of the Fool. Pure will is his instrument and intuition his battle plan.

The Symbolic Emperor
The Emperor is the power of Aries, the first emanation from the Empress and the self-assertiveness of the will and power over instincts. The cubic throne against the backdrop of mountains is his anchor in the physical world, the body and domain of the earth mother, over which the masculine will attempts to assert its power. The organization of his power is impressed upon the powerful feminine unconscious. He is a spiritual warrior and his truth ultimately triumphs over physical power alone.

Guided Imagery
'Wandering in the harsh and barren wasteland, you come across a gigantic but deserted throne at the edge of a cool, clear

lake. You climb into it, feel its authority and survey the view. Reflected in the gold around you you see symbols of power: a sceptre and orb, as well as weapons of battle. Suddenly you hear the sound of adoring subjects surrounding the throne and see readied armies preparing for battle awaiting your commands. They need your presence and direction, which you disperse with no hesitation. How do you feel being needed and respected for your power and wisdom?'

The Meaning
Using will to conquer your unconsciousness. Recognizing the source of your strength of personality in mothering and nurturing. Confidence and creativity brought by taking chances. Following your own path and discovering the Way. Stability and power through taking on responsibility. Conviction with authority.

Affirmation
'I have the willpower, discipline and ambition to take the first steps on the path to meet my highest goals.'

THE HIEROPHANT
Magus of the Eternal

Arcanum Five
The sign Taurus
Key Word: Religion
Hebrew Letter: Vau

THE HIEROPHANT

Enthroned on a cube between two columns, the Hierophant wearing a triple-tiered crown holds a sceptre surmounted by three crosses in his left hand and with his half-closed right he gives a benediction to two tonsured figures kneeling at his feet. Because he sits within a different temple from the High Priestess, he is the power of organized religion as she symbolizes the esoteric. Before him are crossed keys and pentacles, indicating his domain over the physical world.

The Symbolic High Priest
The Hierophant has been called the Abbot, the High Priest and the Pope in his role as spiritual lawgiver. He is symbolic of the sign Taurus, the physical foundation of the spiritual quest, and is paired with, as he emanates from, the lunar High Priestess. He represents the integration of the concealed doctrine and its outer manifestation in his gesture and crossed keys, as he reveals daily the sacred aspects of life. Righteousness and

36

rigidity are his inherent characteristics, yet he bestows grace to the bowing mendicants at his feet. He is not religion, but its means of manifestation. The triple crown and crossed sceptre symbolize his ascent through the physical, emotional and mental worlds and his power of redemption.

Guided Imagery

'Entering the dark and monumental halls of the ancient temple you feel overwhelmed and intimidated. A light glows from the far end of the colonnade as you behold a gigantic throne from which emanates a sense of spiritual power and piety. You mingle with a crowd of mendicants searching for blessing and grace, yet are singled out to receive the benediction of the crowned figure commanding the throne. What strikes you as remarkable is the contrasting shadow behind this figure, as though he draws his power from the darkness. He is a repository of wisdom and offers forgiveness, and unites pagan feelings with the clarity and light of Christ.'

The Meaning

The ability to transform raw material into spiritual energies by acknowledging higher authority. Marriage or other higher alliances, mercy and benediction through servitude to higher powers. The value of ceremony and symbolism in mundane affairs. Art through practicality. Teaching and the ability to learn.

Affirmation

'I am inspired and guided by my highest wisdom for the greatest good, finding it within myself and the world.'

THE LOVERS
*Children of the Voice, Oracle
of the Mighty Gods*

Arcanum Six
The sign Gemini
Key Word: Emotional Life
Hebrew Letter: Zain

As a regent of the radiant sun, a winged figure from the clouds protects and nurtures a naked primordial couple in Eden who are flanked by the Tree of Knowledge of Good and Evil and a fertile tree of life bearing twelve fruits. They are youthful and innocent, but have not yet consummated their union. The serpent beckons their attention as the world stretches out behind them to the highest mountains in the distance.

The Symbolic Lovers
The Lovers are the communicative qualities of Gemini in their dual role as Eve and Adam or sister and brother, signifying the two forms of male-female relationship which integrate in every couple and within each individual of both sexes. The female-male duality emanates from the One above, and by implication the path of knowledge requires the reuniting of these apparent opposites. The feminine powers of the unconscious and of time nurture and yet conquer all relationships. Desire may

38

put knowledge and fertility in their right relationship as the focus of cosmic forces above us.

Guided Imagery
'The garden stretches as far as you can see, lush and fertile in every way. Plants blossom and fruit before your eyes, and everything is lit with golden sunlight. In a radiant clearing are two trees, one with twelve different ripe fruits hanging from its branches, the other beautiful beyond description but containing a glittering green serpent. The allure of the trees is difficult to resist, and the promise of knowingness emanates from the serpent, making his presence quite seductive. An image of your ideal partner appears before you, encouraging your fantasies and hopes of perfect union. By letting go your resistance, your wishes will be answered.'

The Meaning
Higher aspects of yourself can be the best mediators. Value the process more than the outcome. Choices between outer and inner worth. Control brings higher awareness. Attraction and vacillation may only be resolved by decision and commitment. Friendly or brotherly-sisterly communication, friendship between opposites united in knowledge; intellectual flexibility.

Affirmation
'I love both the feminine and the masculine parts of myself, and wish to share my integration with others by demonstrating how accepting I can be.'

THE CHARIOT
Child of the Powers of the Waters, Lord of the Triumph of Light

Arcanum Seven
The sign Cancer
Key Word: Magic
Hebrew Letter: Cheth

THE CHARIOT.

The handsome and upright man rides in his war chariot drawn by one light and one dark sphinx. The double wand of his powerful will, which tames the instincts and emotions, is pointing upwards from within the chariot. His helmet and the canopy above his head are decorated with stars, as are his shoulders with crescent moons, and his zodiacal belt indicates his celestial and heavenly purpose. On the front of the square chariot body is painted a winged solar disc and a lingum symbol linking female and male energies. The walled city away from which he travels indicates the world of form he leaves behind in his quest to dominate the divine realm within himself.

The Symbolic Chariot
The Chariot is the dominance of awakened mind over the instincts and emotions symbolized by the sphinxes drawing him and the walled city he has left behind. His Cancerian

task is to break out of the captivity of feelings and to conquer in the outer world that which he has overcome in his inner world. The cubic shape of the chariot and its four canopy supports symbolize the body and its fourfold nature (see page 72). The starry canopy and the black and white sphinxes signify our contradictory animal and divine nature and refer to the celestial hierarchy of constellations which reflect earthly actions. The secret wisdom is attained by warring with and overcoming our lower nature and bringing the resultant unified being into the world of form.

Guided Imagery
'You are a warrior of light, wearing shining armour emblazoned with crescent moons and strange glyphs, climbing into your gleaming chariot. You leave the darkened city of your birth behind as you must respect and embrace the earthly realm where you were dominated by mother and senses. The sphinxes drawing your cubic chariot are powerfully pulling in opposite directions, awaiting your controlling will. As you take the reigns, they unite with great force along the clear path until they ascend towards the twinkling stars above. The starry canopy of your vehicle disappears against the heavens, and you accept that their and your place is to merge with the constellations. Knowing the loving core within you, you ascend to the place of higher understanding.'

The Meaning
Understanding from emotional difficulty. The path of renouncing earthly power in favour of personal integration. Conquering instincts and directing oneself wisely. Obeying the higher level of being within ourselves. Irreversible power acknowledged from above.

Affirmation
'I conquer my instincts and emotions with the intentions of my higher self and achieve physical goals.'

STRENGTH
*Daughter of the Flaming Sword,
Leader of the Lion*

Arcanum Eight
The sign Leo
Key Word: Self-Consciousness
Hebrew Letter: Teth ט

An innocent young woman, wearing a crown and belt of flowers, closes the jaws of a lion. Above her head is suspended a lemniscate, the infinity symbol of the holy spirit. She has yoked the savage beast with a chain of flowers, showing that she has subdued her animalistic passions and overcome the lower aspects of her nature in favour of her higher self.

The Symbolic Strength
Strength or Fortitude is symbolized by the sign Leo in its virginal and moral self-consciousness and spirituality, albeit in a primarily unconscious form. The lemniscate echoes the Magician in its taming of the self. Strength emanates from a life of contemplation, of integrating with the chain of souls, shown by the flowers. Some relate her to Diana, with her arrows of organization and direction of creativity, conquering the destructive influence of desire and sexuality. The divine law of love and strength are bound to prevail over the wild instincts.

Guided Imagery

'In the hot and rocky place you wander without water and sustenance. As the only way out is through a narrow canyon, you enter and see a ferocious lion blocking your way. To run or hide would be fruitless, so the only solution is to walk slowly and calmly towards the lion, trusting your good heart to tame the savage beast. Your confidence affects him as he moves to you, not in anger or violence, but as a friend. He brushes against your leg like a house cat and presents his head to be stroked. You realize that in your centredness you have made a potential enemy into an ally and source of spiritual strength.'

The Meaning

The courage to face fears bring great personal power. Spirit is capable of overcoming unconscious blocks and repression. Conquering the self is the greatest battle. Action, success and honour, courage and consciousness of self.

Affirmation

'My greatest fears and weakness provide the energy which enables me to express my higher self and reach my dreams.'

THE HERMIT
Prophet of the Eternal, Magus
of the Voice of Power

Arcanum Nine
The sign Virgo
Key Word: Searching Wisdom
Hebrew Letter: Yod

On the apex of a mountain chain, a cloaked and bearded old man carrying a long staff and extending a lamp illuminated by a star searches for the truth. Although he is alone in his meditation on the natural world, he brings enlightenment and openness to the barren reaches of the earth and initiates the journey across the valley of life.

The Symbolic Hermit
The Hermit expresses the Virgo qualities of purity and discrimination, as his simplicity is transformed into understanding through maturity. His lonely search is symbolized in some decks by the partial obscuring of the lantern, which implies obedience to the hidden doctrine, but it may also mean recognition and wisdom from stellar influences. The mysteries are protected from the uninitiated by the isolation and loneliness of its practitioners.

Guided Imagery

'Trekking across the harsh mountain range you reach a small but high plateau which presents a magnificent view over the surrounding countryside. Suspended on top between a barren tree and a fruitful tree is a rainbow of silk, flapping in the wind, through which the rising sun shines, illuminating you in spectral colours. In this quiet and isolated place your mood instantly changes from hopelessness to positive expectation, and you feel as though you have found the inner strength in your meditative isolation to continue on to your highest goals.'

The Meaning

Meditation and the inward path allow everything to be seen more clearly. Hidden meanings may be discovered through perseverance and openness. Service and renunciation bring wisdom. Naivety and prudishness. Circumspection, caution and distance from feelings. Purity and discrimination.

Affirmation

'I look within for the guidance of my higher self to elevate my moods and direct me to the light.'

THE WHEEL OF FORTUNE
Lord of the Forces of Life

Arcanum Ten
The planet Jupiter
Key Word: Life
Hebrew Letter: Kaph ⟍

A sphinx armed with a sword is astride the Wheel of Fortune, rotating perpetually like the eternal cycle of life in the universe. Magical symbols identify the eight spokes of the wheel, and the letters spelling ROTA, a transliteration of TAROT, and the Hebrew name of God – yod hé vau hé – are inscribed around the rim of the wheel. The Egyptian god Typhon rises up the left side and the snake of time falls down the right side of the figure. In the corners sit the four beasts of Ezekiel or the Apocalypse, the bull, the lion, the eagle and the man, all opening the books of the law.

The Symbolic Wheel of Fortune
The planet Jupiter transcends time as it rules higher mind and the spiritual life. The half-lion, half-human sphinx symbolizes equilibrium derived from integrating the lower animal nature with the higher mind. The Indian wheel of *samsara* is the cycle of birth, death and rebirth upon which all souls are

crucified, bound by the mechanics of the zodiac, symbolized by the four sacred beasts, which are also the four signs of the fixed cross – Taurus, Leo, Scorpio and Aquarius. The creatures of time, Typhon and the snake, show that time runs the wheel. The only liberation lies within the centre, in the domain of the self.

Guided Imagery

'Rotating solemnly through the starry expanses of space, the eternal wheel carries the life principle round and round. Wild beasts, creatures of beauty and power, and humans crawl perpetually around the wheel and attempt to fight against gravity and climb along one of the eight spokes into the centre, which glows with the white light of salvation. The need to hold on tightly to avoid falling off counteracts the desire to move quickly towards the goal. The need to touch and crawl over the threatening or repulsive animals makes you feel ill and under constant threat. Suddenly you let go of your grasp which, instead of spinning you into the void, guides you toward the magical temple at the centre of life. By releasing, you find peace.'

The Meaning

Understanding the process of time brings a greater integration with the forces of destiny. Taking chances leads to success, but also to occasional failure, in keeping with the dynamics of the wheel. The laws of karma bring wisdom and peace. Good fortune, success, luck, unpredictable influences.

Affirmation

'As I experience the fluctuations of my physical, emotional and mental life and accept the process completely, I am enabled to manifest my full spiritual potential.'

JUSTICE
Daughter of the Lords of Truth,
Ruler of the Balance

Arcanum Eleven
The sign Libra
Key Word: Truth
Hebrew Letter: Lamed

Crowned Justice sits between her pillars holding a scales for weighing guilt or innocence and a sword to administer her verdict. The card is similar to the Egyptian god Osiris weighing souls before their trip to the underworld. The principle of balance and adjustment implies the recognition of a higher moral and spiritual order which must be considered against the mundane life where such considerations are of little importance.

The Symbolic Justice
The Libran goddess Justice shows that the feminine principle is a source of balance and integration. As the goddess Astraea, she personifies virtue and the recognition of partnership and relationship. The suspended pans carry the opposing aspects of the self while the scales themselves mediate between them, signifying the third principle or viewpoint which arbitrates between them. An awareness of one's own inner imbalances

48

must precede integration with others or outer reality. Partners are either defined or limited by the laws of their relationship, and the future of their lives bears witness to their ability to make just choices.

Guided Imagery
'Entering the massive and impressive halls of black and white marble it is clear that you will be judged by superior powers which care not for your emotional stances or excuses. A cold sweat arises at the realization that this place is a house of justice but also of retribution and death. Above the scarlet dais is suspended a gigantic golden scales, delicately poised in space, awaiting the breath of a feather to disturb its equilibrium. You are afraid to breathe for fear that you will be responsible for the terrible onslaught of divine right. Realizing that you do not have a fear of the truth brings a clearing of the air and an alignment with these superior intelligences.'

The Meaning
Deliberation leads to correct choices. The recognition that imbalance originates within, and the restoration of balance also begins within. Harmony, equality, discrimination, justice, getting just deserts, legal affairs.

Affirmation
'I am balanced and able to understand the outer manifestations of my inner issues, and subsequently to take the correct action with honour.'

THE HANGED MAN
Spirit of the Mighty Waters

Arcanum Twelve
The planet Neptune and the
element Water
Key Word: Sacrifice
Hebrew Letter: Mem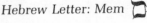

THE HANGED MAN.

A smiling golden-haired young man with a halo hangs from living branches shaped like a tau cross. His legs form a cross and his arms extend behind his back, making an upside down triangle – his whole body makes the alchemical sulphur symbol signifying the eternal fire. His countenance suggests suspended animation rather than martyrdom.

The Symbolic Hanged Man
Water symbolizes the emotional life and the Hanged Man is pure unconsciousness. He appears to be sacrificed by those on earth, but is in reality showing his allegiance to the powers above. Neptune is the visionary psychic domain which is more vivid than reality – spiritual humanity is trapped by reality, crucified on the cross of matter. The Hebrew letter tau is the saturnine quality of time and signifies the entrapment of the world. The pure soul understands and loves its boundaries like an adoring mother loves her child.

50

Guided Imagery

'Feeling trapped by the limitations of your own conscious image of the universe, you wish to move beyond these restrictions. The meditative position you adopt is a headstand without supporting arms, and once you achieve this position you begin to feel the transformation taking place. What were before glittering stars in the unlimited heavens above, now seem dense and lifeless, while the gravitational bond of the solid and impermeable earth below becomes alive with vibrant energy and illumination. You can feel your head radiating an other-worldly light in your ultimate enchantment.'

The Meaning

The secrets of divination and prophecy lie within the self and through communication with the feminine and unconscious aspects of the self. Wisdom through sacrifice, trials, being circumspect.

Affirmation

'I relinquish my attachments and fears in the faith that this sacrifice of invalid patterns will open me to a new life.'

DEATH
Child of the Great Transformers, Lord of the Gates of Death

Arcanum Thirteen
The sign Scorpio
Key Word: Death
Hebrew Letter: Nun

A mounted skeleton in armour carries his black banner emblazoned with an inverted red rose through a field containing a fallen king, a sleeping maiden, a kneeling lad and a praying prelate awaiting his doom. Nearby the tranquil river of life flows by and through the twin towers on the horizon the sun's last rays blaze.

The Symbolic Death
Death overshadows all aspects of life and is omnipresent in its process of testing, separation and renewal. Death's mount shows the animal and instinctive reality of dying, while his banner signifies the eternal qualities of life that emerge from apparent destruction. Despite the finality of transformation, the river of life flows on and the sun of immortality shines through the gateway symbolizing the dualism of this ultimate challenge.

Guided Imagery
'Standing in a state of cold and still detachment, your body seems to fall away. Its heaviness, caused by worldly burdens and emotional attachments, begins to lessen as its feelings leave. The long journey begins, initially with sadness and regret, but gradually the glimmering soul detaches from the body and rises, seeking the white light above and beyond. Upon this star your soul's journey is now focused, the inner light overshadowing the outer pain of living. The release is a godsend, a rest from holding on to decaying patterns, the start of a new adventure. You can see the small physical world left behind, while the greater world of spirit beckons. There nothing but darkness, here eternal sun. You have been crucified within your body, but now you are free.'

The Meaning
Loss, change and renewal. Breakdown leading to transformation. Releasing possessions, ideas or relationships or releasing ways of seeing oneself or others.

Affirmation
'I leave my needs and relationships behind and seek the higher light within myself. The more I let go, the freer and more luminous I become.'

TEMPERANCE
Daughter of the Reconcilers,
Bringer Forth of Life

Arcanum Fourteen
The sign Sagittarius
Key Word: Integration
Hebrew Letter: Samekh

A heavenly winged angel with a solar disc headband pours the mercurial life substance from a golden to a silver chalice. Upon her flowing robes is a triangle within a square. One foot rests upon the earth and the other in the life-giving water, at the intersection of which many plants and flowers grow. Stretching away from this fertile source curves a road leading to a crown-shaped light blazing beyond the hills.

The Symbolic Temperance
Temperance is the quality which characterizes the integration of the lower fertile animal instincts and the higher need for transcendental consciousness. Sagittarius is the moral aspiration and craving to understand which leads the soul beyond sensual satisfaction to the higher psychic and spiritual life. The transformative Aquarian fluid shows the necessary flow of masculine conscious and feminine unconscious qualities which together create the integrated Self. The vessels

are wombs of the potential creativity of our outer and inner being which require interaction and the exchange of energies. The goddess Persephone similarly bridged life and death by nourishing the souls below preceding their rebirth. The goal of the process of integration is beyond the horizon, in the domain of the higher being.

Guided Imagery

'Arising from the Death of my clarity, from within the golden vessel you spiral slowly towards its mouth, and arch out into the clear, fresh air, only to be caught by another silvery grail. Your fluidity arises from the crystal lake and emerges onto the fertile and damp ground. You are surrounded by lush and beautiful plants, reeds and flowery stalks which grow upwards towards the blue sky above. You feel drawn to follow the meandering stream to its source beyond the mountains, in the exalted realm where sky and earth intermingle. Your unity lies above and beyond you, yet its feeling always exists within when you achieve and recognize your natural balance.'

The Meaning

Finding a balance between outer and inner moderation defines new limits. Life moves perpetually through phases of light and dark, active and passive. Identification with the flow. Patience, self-control and accommodation are required for integration. Circumspection despite physical demands. Psyche and body find a path of integration.

Affirmation

'I integrate and blend the diverse polarities of my life to create balance, unity and harmony in creating who I am and manifesting what I do.'

THE DEVIL
Lord of the Gates of Matter,
Child of the Forces of Time

Arcanum Fifteen
The sign Capricorn
Key Word: Materialism
Hebrew Letter: Ayin ע

THE DEVIL .

The horned goat with batlike wings and an inverted pentangle on his forehead raises one hand in devilish benediction and with the other points a phallic torch toward the ground. Upon his navel sits a hermetic caduceus symbol instead of sexual organs. Chained to his cubic altar of grey stone are two small figures, a male and female with horns and tails, reminding us of the bestial and unconscious natures of Adam and Eve after the Fall.

The Symbolic Devil
Capricorn is the corruption of mechanist materialism and the enchainment of temptation. The god Pan requires indulgence and wild abandonment to the lowest instincts, and the chains show the bondage resulting from the worship of such inferior energies. Weak and corruptible humanity signified by the two figures is trapped and dominated by this masked Devil who gives false benediction and demeans the flame of

spiritual understanding. He is the tempting Guardian of the Threshold, past whom the initiate must pass on the route to enlightenment.

Guided Imagery

'The dreary and dank cave smells of rotten animal carcasses and sulphurous caverns below. Seeing a dim light flashing ahead, you enter a subterranean chamber only to find you have been imprisoned by a great black beast, emblazoned with a flaming pentangle on his forehead. He offers the temptations of the flesh and worldly possessions in exchange for your immortal soul. You are punished almost to the point of accepting his offer, but suddenly a ray of light from a tiny opening in the chamber helps you realize that the material world is an illusion of which you are a part but which need not imprison you.'

The Meaning

Overcoming the attractions of the physical world of the senses. The principle of self-centredness. Relationships to money and power. Excessive materialism prevents psychological growth. Difficulties caused by the demands and needs of the lower desires of the self.

Affirmation

'I will transcend the chaos of my darkest fears and transform my weaknesses and vulnerabilities into a clear channel of light penetrating through the gloom.'

THE TOWER
Lord of the Hosts of the Mighty

Arcanum Sixteen
The planet Mars
Key Word: The Fall
Hebrew Letter: Peh

A male and female figure are falling from a desolate tower, also called the House of God, which is being struck by lightning. The three windows are grouped with one higher than the other two, showing that the physical and emotional worlds are reconciled in the higher spiritual domain. The crown of the tower, which signifies spirituality as seen in the aura, and various bits of debris shower down from the violent event.

The Symbolic Tower
The Martian energy of the tower is shattered by forced change, made manifest by the Scorpionic thunderbolt, which is both fate and forceful spirituality. The tower may represent the physical world or intellectual structures which we have erected, as well as the body and its state of health. Originally it was symbolic of the Fall of Adam and Eve or the destruction of the Tower of Babel. In either case the female and male figures are thrust apart, possibly through the sexual tensions

of the phallic monument. Past patterns are shattered and the creative effort to modify them often requires the sacrifice of what formerly seemed secure. The twenty-two flaming yods (Hebrew letter meaning work) show that from destruction come the forces of creativity and rebirth. The spirit of chaos rules the apparent order of the physical world.

Guided Imagery
'Amidst the steep and treacherous hills you approach the dark tower, immense in its solidity and strength. A wild and windy storm rages through the valleys, but orange fires burn within, illuminating its barred windows like portals into a furnace making gold from base metals. Suddenly a vivid shaft of zig-zagging lightning shatters the gloom and blasts the top of the tower from its base, spewing twenty-two flaming embers and tossing two brilliantly dressed figures into the night sky. It is difficult to know whether they are escaping bondage or losing their security, such is the shock of the storm. You see them magically land, as though cushioned by their capes and velvet clothes. The storm abates and sunrise brings peace to the smoking ruin. You contemplate what you have seen.'

The Meaning
Total change signalled by the end of previous patterns, leading to new beginnings. Unexpected disruptions are caused when attempting to protect oneself, leading to feelings of vulnerability. An inability to look at inner unrest and suppressed anger. Past relationships are abandoned and changes of opinion prevent reconciliation. Downfall, losing everything, violence, sexual domination, insecurity.

Affirmation
'Sudden realizations about inadequate past ideas and patterns free me instantly from self-created limitations and physically binding circumstances.'

THE STAR
Daughter of the Firmament,
Dweller Between the Waters

Arcanum Seventeen
The sign Aquarius
Key Word: Astral Religion
Hebrew Letter: Tzaddi ꜩ

A radiant star of eight rays is surrounded by seven lesser stars. A young and beautiful naked woman kneels on the land but her foot is in the water. She pours the waters of life onto the land and in the sea, providing life-giving sustenance to both. In a tree behind her sits a bird.

The Symbolic Star
The Aquarian symbolism of the star is idealistic, utopian and perfect in form, like the unveiled truth she represents. The maiden guides the goals of humanity and shines with ethereal light. Progressive spiritual evolution and the necessity for grounding integrate, symbolized by the two vessels and her stance astride water and land. The central star is Sirius, worshipped by the Egyptians as the sun of our sun, and the seven stars of the Great Bear are the governing esoteric spirits of our universe, just as the star symbolizes the soul. Astrological influences nurture human expectations. New

conceptions and opportunities arise through the feminine desire for synthesis.

Guided Imagery

'Wandering through the barren valley at sunset, you pray for some sign of life. Turning past a small hill with a tree surmounting it, you hear a bird calling and see a cool, clear pond surrounded by fertility everywhere, in the water, at its edge and in the proliferation of wildlife around it. The intersection between the water and land has a magical radiance, and the surface of the water glistens like gold and silver. The atmosphere is tranquil and quiet, and you feel nurtured, supported and full of eternal hope for the future without knowing why. As the sky darkens you notice the gigantic star overhead, surrounded by seven others, dancing across the heavens. Suddenly you know that you are protected by forces beyond yourself.'

The Meaning

Barren areas of your life may be fertilized by seeing the power above. Prayer brings release and accesses the depths of your psyche. Faith and hope guide the present. A symbol of the collective unconscious. Questing for realization. The magical power of astrology representing higher powers. Hope and expectation.

Affirmation

'I am a living, breathing star radiating pure energies and giving sustenance to myself and others through the inspiration of my light.'

THE MOON
Ruler of Flux and Reflux

Arcanum Eighteen
The sign Pisces
Key Word: Astrological Nature
Hebrew Letter: Qoph ק

Between two dark towers on either side of a path wandering into the distance are a dog and a wolf baying at the crescent moon overhead. The face of the waxing moon gleams as it cries fertilizing dewdrops below. A large red lobster emerges from the lapping waters of the unconscious onto dry land.

The Symbolic Moon
Pisces symbolizes the psychic and sacrificial qualities of the moon goddess. It was believed that her tears fertilized the land, and the duality of her nature is shown by the two towers and baying animals, representing the unconscious voices we all hear through emotional veils. The towers are rigid symbols of masculine, phallic consciousness, through which the unconscious penetrates as through a transparent veil. The moon counsels balanced feelings as an equilibrating path between the dualistic upper and lower worlds. The pond is the past, stagnant below us, and out of which our higher self emerges as the lobster.

Guided Imagery
'The boat crossed the dark lake and ground ashore – it had been mystically guided here. Walking up the shore, the beginning of a path below is reflected in a glowing cleft in the cloudy sky overhead. As you walk up the gradual incline the clouds part and through the heavy air the brilliant crescent moon shines its fertilizing rays down onto your expectant face. The path ahead meanders between two sinister and dark towers, standing sentinel over the only way ahead. As you move carefully, you are shocked to hear the baying of a wild dog and a wolf echoing through the mist. Your need to continue overcomes your fears at what could lie ahead. As you keep unwaveringly along the path and simply acknowledge but resist the dangers lurking you see, over a rise, the road ahead, stretching clearly towards the distant horizon.'

The Meaning
Deceptions arouse strong emotions and must be clarified. Past influences stand in the way of progress and development. Meditation and inner light compensate for outer illusions and unrealistic expectations from the world. Obscurity and trickery. Warnings from others and from intuitions. A multitude of influences can lead to confusion and incorrect priorities.

Affirmation
'I value both my positive and negative feelings as expressions of the world around me, and accept their enrichment and fertilization.'

THE SUN
Lord of the Fire of the World

Arcanum Nineteen
The Sun
Key Word: Visible Experience
Hebrew Letter: Resh ר

THE SUN .

The brilliant noonday sun casts its rays down into an enclosed garden, surrounded by tall sunflowers. A young naked child is mounted on a white horse and carries a scarlet banner. The light of the world carried by children reflects the creative child within us. Consciousness and spirit penetrate all enclosures to bring awareness and knowledge.

The Symbolic Sun
The sun is the source of spiritual energy, creativity and life, expressing itself as a beneficent and protective god above us. The image has also been seen as Sirius, the dog star of the Egyptians shown in the Star, bestowing fertility through the goddess Isis. The more powerful the draw or demands of the physical world, the more important is penetration of high spiritual wisdom. The integration of above and below, happens within the yearly cycle of the zodiac signs, bringing the alternation of life and death on earth.

Guided Imagery
'Within the masonry enclosure the cold morning air brings a sense of barrenness. But when the sun rises above the wall's blockage, a supernatural warmth arises gradually and warms and nurtures your body and brings excitement and inspiration to your mind. A feeling of belonging to this powerful and yet totally controlled being above echoes the entrapment of your body and the acceptance of your destiny, written in the skies but enacted through the alliance with your free will to act. A mystical child, taming a wild horse which bursts into the courtyard, makes you think of your ability to control the unconscious impulses you have by the recognition of your conscious control over the world. What you think is what you are.'

The Meaning
The awakening of the child within brings new life, joy and inspiration. Higher influences bring freedom from rigid structures and the demands of the physical world. The merging of two people requires a binding and integration of their higher ideals. Experiencing life in the sun activates inner truth and increases your self worth.

Affirmation
'I understand my physical limitations but look to heaven to find the inspiration to trust and live with my inner child. Personal growth comes through relinquishing my rigid personal boundaries.'

JUDGMENT
Spirit of Primal Fire

Arcanum Twenty
The planet Pluto and the
element Fire
Key Words: Regeneration and
Resurrection
Hebrew Letter: Shin

An angel appears from the clouds blowing a bannered trumpet bearing a cross. Below it the dead are rising from their watery graves. In the foreground stand a triumvirate of man, child and woman with outstretched hands, as though welcoming the resurrection. The Biblical Last Judgment portrays the resurrection of the souls of those blessed in the eyes of God, a concept depicted here.

The Symbolic Judgment
The function of the element fire is to provide heat and energy when controlled, and total destruction when rampant. The force of life here needs the degeneration and breakdown into component parts before resurrection can take place. Only the death of obsolete life structures and beliefs allows the rebirth into higher, more transcendent states of consciousness. The coffins are the body, in which we are imprisoned until liberated at death, and they float upon the surface of the

unconscious awaiting the awakening. Integration between female and male brings the inner child to birth and allows unification. The angel above is Gabriel giving a celestial justification to the reality of resurrection.

Guided Imagery

'Among the snow-capped mountain fastnesses and the enclosed valley, ringed with drifting eagles, you come upon a plain somewhere between earth and heaven. It is the graveyard of mortal souls, but contains the great potential of rebirth. The grey sky and barren ground begins a profound transformation before your eyes. The earth breaks up of its own accord, and long-closed coffin lids push the surface of the ground away, as the sky turns brilliant blue and the plants and flowers push through the ground and reach toward the sky. The time of resurrection is at hand, and the souls of the dead stretch and pay homage to the heavenly host above, who symbolize their rebirth. The joy of creation and transcendence reigns over the valley.'

The Meaning

Forgiveness and repentance bring about resurrection into a new life. Making central choices reinforces the correctness of your spiritual direction. Completion and resolution can only create redemption. Changes of position and beliefs. Rebirth. Being judged reflects your judgments of others. Success comes through decisiveness.

Affirmation

'I release my feelings of bodily bondage and sense the awakening of my soul as my integration process brings a perpetual flowering in its wake.'

THE WORLD
Great One of the Night of Time

Arcanum Twenty-One
The planet Saturn
Key Word: Time
Hebrew Letter: Tau ת

The four creatures of the Apocalypse and Ezekiel's vision are grouped around the oval garland of flowers bound above and below with crossed red ribbons. Within a maiden dances, enwrapped with violet silk and carrying a wand in each hand. She is the scarlet woman dancing the dance of time and eternity, spiralling and twirling through life as a blithe spirit.

The Symbolic World
The spiralling bonds of Saturn define and limit physical space and time, the oval vessel within which the dance of life takes place. Fertility and sexuality exist to propagate the universe and create the manifest world, providing the players in the divine plan. The opposing crosses are the duality and conflict engendered by the existence of life, yet the battle takes place within. The spiritual process of discovery begins with the Fool and ends here in the heavens, where its markers are astrological as well as astronomical, religious and secular.

The world is the father of form and also takes away what he bestows upon all forms of intelligence. That is his function and the ultimate mystery.

Guided Imagery
'Drifting through the dark and cold vastness of space, piloting against unmeasurable and unimaginable clusters of galaxies and backgrounds of the void, you enter a sacred domain. A spiral of stars swirls in an oval form around and around, its boundaries clearly alive with the animals, objects and beings of the zodiac belt. Their presence can be felt, as though instead of stars they are the bodies of these mythic creatures from whom our lives are created. At the centre of their swirling movement, instead of the outer coldness is a warmth, a golden glow arising from a dancing goddess, spinning and leaping in supremely beautiful arcs, wearing only a glimmer of a violet silken cloth draped around her as the wings of an angel. As you come closer, she glides near and whispers in your ear the key to enlightenment.'

The Meaning
Our sense of well-being originates from the ability to understand the whole; the need for integration of personal and collective; encouraging self-trust and dominance; the primary principle of individuation; expressions of identification in the world; creating or building a new vision of yourself.

Affirmation
'I am a co-creator of the world, and know that I will be nurtured and supported by it as I acknowledge my identity with all its actions.'

THE MAGICIAN.

5 · THE MINOR ARCANA

The major arcana cards are archetypal symbols acting in a transformative manner. They describe the symbols at the heart of the archetypal ways of being within us rather than their personifications as others, or their manifestations as events in the outer world. The minor arcana cards represent the outer manifestations of the archetypal principles embodied in the major arcana cards, symbols of the way the archetypes act in our lives. The minor arcana cards are divided into four functions of consciousness or personality types: the pentacles (sensation and the element earth), wands (intuition and the element fire), swords (thinking and the element air) and cups (feeling and the element water).

Until this century the sixteen court cards, which are similar to the face cards in a playing card deck with the addition of four pages or princesses, and the forty numbered minor arcana cards, were indistinguishable from a playing card deck. The court cards had similar images of kings, queens, knights and pages holding the symbols of the four suits. The minor arcana cards had only numbers of pentacles, swords, cups or wands corresponding to the card numbers, like the pips on playing cards. Often their patterns were geometric and like mandalas. There was no divinatory information at all in either the court cards or minor arcana. Waite states that while the major arcana belong to the divine dealings of philosophy, the minor arcana remain in the domain of fortune-telling. Indeed he calls them the 'Lesser Arcana' and warns us not to be taken in by the designs of the cards when they seem to exceed their stated divinatory meaning (*The Pictorial Key to the Tarot*, pp. 168–9).

In a general sense there is a hierarchy of strength and value in the three classes of tarot cards. The twenty-two major arcana cards, being archetypes, are the strongest; the sixteen court cards are personifications or character types representing the archetypal energies which are next strongest; and the cards numbered from ace to ten are a series or sequence of events or experiences through which the archetypes come into being in day to day life situations. The tarot embodies three levels of operation in the following scheme:

Major Arcana = archetypal influences = depth psychology work

Court Cards = character or personality types = sub-personality work

Numbered Cards = experiences and events = divinatory work

Archetypal influences are the deep, pervasive and powerful forces which shape us from the inside and only eventually become conscious and manifest as outer events. Work with the personality, or its component subpersonalities, involves identifying, communicating with and differentiating the various ways we perceive ourself and act. Experiences and events in our lives are the ground of action and being which serves to teach us about the soul.

The distinction is important because it is extremely easy in our process of transformation to lose sight of the level at which we should be concentrating our energies. While there is almost always a combination of influences from all three levels, and an understanding of their relative importance and potential integration, their distinct qualities should be clear to us, otherwise we may place undue importance upon minor aspects of our lives and overlook the more significant, but less obvious, deeper archetypal influences which are also in action.

71

THE FOUR ELEMENTAL SUITS

The minor arcana is divided into four suits: wands, swords, cups and pentacles. The suits are symbolic of the ways we function in life. We sense and perceive the world: we receive information, and form inner intuitions or develop its potentials: we attempt to understand and adjust to the world: and we evaluate whether a given situation is pleasurable or not. These psychological functions are similar to and derived from the four elements from which the Platonic philosophers, alchemists and astrologers believed the universe was made.

Four-foldness is a universal symbol for the growth of consciousness and the psychological individuation process of identification (discovery of our being) and differentiation (recognition of our uniqueness within the collective) which we experience in life. The need for connection and isolation, for companionship and individuality, are often conflicting drives within our selves, and these are symbolized by the four suits and their symbolic devices. The true individual is able to become conscious of the roles of the various functions, to differentiate their varying actions, and to reconcile and integrate their influences. This process begins at birth and is never finished.

The correspondences between suits, elements and psychological types have been made by many commentators, although there are differences of opinion about them. The most satisfying correlation is:

Wands	=	Fire Element	=	Intuition Type
Cups	=	Water Element	=	Feeling Type
Swords	=	Air Element	=	Thinking Type
Pentacles	=	Earth Element	=	Sensation Type

There is a hierarchy of values within the suits, from the pure energy of wands to the dense material of pentacles. Their sequence symbolizes the descent from the spirit (wands) down through the elements to physical manifestation (pentacles) and then the ascent back up through the elements to spiritual enlightenment again. Many commentators see the tarot itself as a symbol of the descent into the realm of the unconscious and the return back to the spiritual domain.

The **suit of wands** corresponds to the element fire, as the image of the Magician's wand or the lightning rod which attracts and grounds lightning bolts. Fire is the first essential form of energy in the universe, emanating from the sun as rays of pure light which create life, yet also are capable of taking life. As the terrestrial form of the sun, fire transforms by destroying the form of its fuel, it dissolves shapes, eliminates boundaries and, while not liquid like water, similarly can break down into the essence qualities. It was believed in ancient times that the universe began as 'cosmic fire' and that the essential, underlying life force or substance within all objects is fire. In daily life the wands are life energy, individuality, insight, power of attainment and struggles, issues of success and failure, politics and commerce.

The **suit of cups** corresponds to the element water. The unusual way in which water flows into the form which contains it, and yet tends to break through all containers, is characteristic of its action. Water is often seen as clear and transparent, but may also be dark, deep, mysterious and extremely dangerous when aroused. Indeed the sea and the night sky were often compared to each other for their ability to generate forms, to excite the imagination and to evoke awe. An image evoked by the cups suit is the quest for the Holy Grail. Duality and the quality of the shadow are inherent in the cup suit. It is water which symbolizes the unconscious, the source of all life, the most liquid, changeable, formless and yet powerful force in our world. The cups are also emotions and feelings, which are rhythmic, changeable, and take their form by whatever forces mould them. By a beautiful metaphor, the element water is symbolized by the cup which contains it. Its contents are understanding and consciousness. Thus the cup may be as evocative empty as full, and symbolic of our ability to contain as well as manage our feelings. In daily life the cups mirror your emotional reality in matters of relationships, feelings, love, sex, romance, family, marriage and children.

The **suit of swords** corresponds to the element air, as the function of swords is to cut through information in the act of discrimination. The element of Air symbolizes the principle of communication, of the relationship of things to each other and to the higher and lower worlds. Air is the expression of pure mind which manifests as perception, self-expression, ideology, compatibility and logic. It is air which brings together, but also which differentiates, criticizes, detaches from and alienates – in this sense it is unpredictable and unstable. In Eastern thought the mind must be stilled before the contemplative process of development can even begin. Images of mind often correlate its control with its capabilities. The mind makes us humane and sympathetic to others, but is also cold and detaches us from human concerns. In daily life the swords indicate the level of consciousness, and are ideas and their fulfilment, versatility, idealistic relationships, movement and changes of stance and mind.

The **suit of pentacles** is associated with the element earth. The pentacles were also called discs or coins, showing their connection with money and value. The pentacle was also the foremost protective talismanic figure in medieval times, thought to ward off evil spirits. It is earth from which all beings in the physical world arise, and is also the body through which our soul experiences the world. In the Christian mystery, the cross symbolizes both the world and the body into which we are incarnated. While the intuitional and thinking functions initiate activity, they must be grounded in reality through the earth element. Earth stabilizes, sustains and defines, and represents our relationship with the tangible world and its boundaries. The ability to accept and work with the physical level is a prerequisite for the journey of enlightenment on the higher spiritual levels. In ancient societies the body was often demeaned as evil or sinful, but its purification is essential to the entire process of integration. In daily life the pentacles show what is happening in external reality – the physical body, money and our ability to use it, property and possessions, our practical and material side which is conservative and industrious. Pentacles are often resistant to change, are loyal and reliable, but can also be pig-headed, stubborn and unfeeling.

CORRELATIONS OF THE MINOR ARCANA

The court cards are associated with the elements and with astrological signs in their function as personifications to be used in tarot, and as symbols of the varying degrees of mastery of levels of consciousness. The wands show intuitive and spiritual consciousness; the swords mental awareness; the cups emotional consciousness; and the pentacles physical consciousness and external reality. In a psychological sense the court cards may be understood as subpersonalities which indicate that a particular level of awareness has been obtained or is being required of us.

In some recent decks the minor arcana are correlated with goddesses, as in the *Secrets of the Tarot* deck by Barbara Walker, author of the *Woman's Encyclopedia of Myths and Secrets.* Within our myths are our archetypal history, enacted by the gods and goddesses. By identifying with these primordial aspects of ourselves and becoming familiar with the myths and their lessons, we see the minor arcana as a series of paths through the collective unconscious.

Crowley considered the court cards to be families of the four elements and their permutations. His correlation is interesting because it shows how the elements function within us, with each element containing aspects of the other three. (Crowley also used the sequence knight, queen, prince and princess instead of the more traditional king, queen, knight and page.) His sequence:

Knight of Wands	=	Fire of Fire	Intuitive intuition
Queen of Wands	=	Water of Fire	Emotional intuition
Prince of Wands	=	Air of Fire	Mental intuition
Princess of Wands	=	Earth of Fire	Physical intuition
Knight of Cups	=	Fire of Water	Intuitive feeling
Queen of Cups	=	Water of Water	Emotional feeling
Prince of Cups	=	Air of Water	Mental feeling
Princess of Cups	=	Earth of Water	Physical feeling
Knight of Swords	=	Fire of Air	Intuitive thinking
Queen of Swords	=	Water of Air	Emotional thinking
Prince of Swords	=	Air of Air	Intellectual thinking
Princess of Swords	=	Earth of Air	Physical thinking

Knight of Pentacles	=	Fire of Earth	Intuitive sensation
Queen of Pentacles	=	Water of Earth	Emotional sensation
Prince of Pentacles	=	Air of Earth	Mental sensation
Princess of Pentacles	=	Earth of Earth	Physical sensation

Within each psychological function are modes which correspond to the other functions. Thus the thoughts expressed by the Swords may arise from feelings in the case of the queen, from intuitions in the case of the knight or king, from the mind itself in the case of Swords and from the physical world or the body in the case of Pentacles.

The court cards are 'modes' of activity, transmitted through individuals around us and our own subpersonalities. When these cards are drawn in a reading, they signify the coming or presence of an individual who carries the archetype from whom we must see and accept its principles, or onto whom we project these qualities, and its presence requires that we exercise the level of mastery indicated.

Astrologically the kings, queens and knights correspond to the twelve sun signs of the zodiac. Astrology recognizes three modes of action and the rank of the card shows which mode is psychologically operative. The kings represent the stable, sustained and fixed mode, the queens the initiatory and instinctive cardinal mode and the knights the changeable, ambiguous and mutable mode. Thus the King of Cups corresponds to the fixed water sign Scorpio, the Queen of Pentacles is the cardinal earth sign Capricorn, and the Knight of Wands is the mutable fire sign Sagittarius. The way we work with such images is that they signal us that the archetype is near, whether in the guise of a person we know, a subpersonality within us of which we are not conscious, or projected onto others around us. This shows us the extent to which we have been able to recognize, identify with or integrate the subpersonality in question. For example, if our anger is aroused on a deep level we are likely to draw the King of Cups, corresponding to the sign Scorpio, which describes anger which has been buried within and sustained on deeper psychological levels.

The page of each suit is the elemental action on the personality level. The Page of Swords is therefore the attribute of thought, the Page of Wands of intuition or energy; the Page of Pentacles of sensuality and physicality; and the Page of Cups of emotion and feeling. Their action is such that it represents the element but without a clearly defined mode of operation. They would be carried by a person who embodied thought, but who might not have specific ideas attractive to you.

The court cards are also aspects of the spiritual principle, although in many decks, including the Rider-Waite deck used in this book, there is an imbalance of male and female personifications. Typically for early decks the male triad of king-knight-page was counterbalanced by the feminine influence of the queen. In some Italian decks the knights were balanced by ladies, and in Crowley's Thoth tarot he uses princes and princesses to make two evenly balanced pairs.

The minor arcana are numbered from ace to ten of each suit and correspond to a process of development from first manifestation to completion of the quality of the element. Some visualize the ten cards as three triangles of operation with the tenth card either as the origin or culmination of the process. A typical scheme for understanding the minor arcana numbers is as follows:

1. The aces are the root or seed of the element.
2. The twos are the element in a pure manifest and uncontaminated way.
3. The threes are the fertilization of the element with an inherent stability.
4. The fours are a solidification and materialization of the element.
5. The fives mobilize and upset the static and stable system and bring change.
6. The sixes are most harmonized, centred and balanced.
7. The sevens are degeneration, weakness and loss of stability.
8. The eights are the unexpected shift caused by an acknowledgement of error.

9. The nines are the crystallization and full impact of the elemental energy in a material way.
10. The tens are the end of the process and the final transformation into rigidity.

Camphausen, Rufus, *Mind Mirror*, pp. 66–8.

The minor arcana are also organized in an astrological fashion, although it is less obvious and only a major factor in the decks influenced by the Golden Dawn tradition, such as the Crowley Thoth tarot. The most common attribution is that each minor arcana card corresponds to one of the thirty-six decanates, ten-degree segments of the twelve astrological signs considered in classical times to be under the domain of specific gods and goddesses. In this model the ace of each suit is the essence of the elemental quality, the 2–3–4 are the three decanates of the cardinal sign of that element; the 5–6–7 are the three decanates of the fixed sign of that element; and the 8–9–10 are the three decanates of the mutable sign of that element. Each suit is therefore a progression through the signs in each element in their natural order. The strength of this correlation is that in renaissance Italy many churches and other buildings were decorated with astrological frescos depicting the images of the decans, which were seen to have magical powers.

THE SUIT OF WANDS

The Wands are the element fire and the psychological function of intuition.

Ace of Wands – Awakening Spirit
A hand emerges from the clouds holding a wand in bloom.

Interpretation
Beginning the quest for self; initiatory energy awaiting direction from above; creativity and invention; understanding one's family and origins; enterprising spirit; money; fortune and inheritance. Reversed: Blind energy without direction; resisting seeing the self; decadence; a clouded joy.

The Wands Cards

Two of Wands – Dominion

A powerful man holds a globe and staff as he looks across the sea from the battlements of a castle above the tranquil countryside. To his left a cube of stone is decorated with roses and lilies in a cross.

Interpretation
Power and integration bring worldly success and riches; conquest and marriage; the isolation of high position; adventure and domination. Reversed: Sadness amidst wealth; wonder and surprise; too much independence; isolation.

Three of Wands – Virtue

A serene personage is seen from the back, watching ships passing from cliffs overlooking the sea. He leans upon one of the three staves growing from the ground.

Interpretation
Personal strength originates with integrity; an alignment of energy and feelings brings powerful action; bringing unconscious contents to awareness leads to cooperation and success; business ventures succeed, especially when dealing with foreign countries. Reversed: Immaturity and a failure of nerve; willpower undirected; an end of troubles through full disclosure; suspension of adversity.

Four of Wands – Completion

A garland suspended from four staves frames two female figures holding bouquets of flowers. Behind them the manor house is protected by an arching bridge.

Interpretation
Stability comes from completing tasks and perfecting the expression of the self; initiative and leadership applied to proper planning leads to success and security; starting a successful venture; prosperity and peace at home; bridging the spiritual and physical worlds. Reversed: Instability caused

by short-sighted goals or a lack of clear objectives; exaggerated expectations; premature expectations; but also, increase and beauty even when reversed.

Five of Wands – Strife
Five youths armed with staves mimic warfare.

Interpretation
Anxiety and frustration are caused by an excess of energy without sufficient direction; holding back from commitment; shallow imitation; struggling for success and riches; possible gain; noble aims without the backup of authority; self-advancement. Reversed: Artificial shows of strength or direction; emptiness and arrogance; optimism without sufficient grounds; lawsuits and trickery.

Six of Wands – Victory
A horseman wearing the laurel wreath of victory and bearing a staff is surrounded by footmen with staves.

Interpretation
Positive expectation and self-confidence brings optimism for long-term goals; expansion of awareness and openness for psychological change; creativity depends upon flexibility of one's world view; the unfolding of the self allows the possibility for new depths and foreign influences into the centre; good news. Reversed: Negative expectations; pessimism caused by difficulties opening up; closing down and suppressing the self; vanity and self-admiration.

Seven of Wands – Valour
A young man standing in a belligerent pose at the edge of a cliff defends himself against six aggressive staves from below.

Interpretation
Standing by beliefs; the courage to resist compromise; enterprise and initiative meet with resistance requiring perseverance; the strength to protect one's own spiritual position;

gaining and defending higher ground. Reversed: Abandoning beliefs; being forced to retire from a stance; caution against indecision.

Eight of Wands – Flight
A squadron of wands fly through the tranquil countryside.

Interpretation
Expansive intuitions require a change of location; modifying direction; optimistically believing in the future; taking prophecies seriously; approaching a speedy end to an issue; love affairs. Reversed: Lack of intuition brings wrong turns and aimlessness; excessive vanity and egotism; domestic disputes.

Nine of Wands – Strength
An injured and forlorn, but powerful figure leans on his staff in front of a wall of staves. His aggressive appearance and stance shows he is facing attack from the east.

Interpretation
Being strong in opposition; facing outer challenges to inner attitudes; perception and instinct join to bring victory; strength created by overcoming physical and energetic opposition from the status quo. Reversed: Being an outsider with unusual ideas; fleeing inner challenges; obstacles behind and in front; adversity.

Ten of Wands – Oppression
A strong man is carrying ten heavy staves towards a small rural village.

Interpretation
Holding back creative powers or self expression through lack of energy or direction; spiritual goals compromised by physical considerations; self-limiting visions of what is possible. Reversed: Contradictory circumstances; jumping to

irrational conclusions; lawsuits with little chance of winning; intrigues.

Page of Wands – Pure Intuition

A courageous young man places his vertical sprouting wand skyward in expectation. His vestments are decorated with salamanders of fire and he is dressed in gold and red, the fiery colours.

Interpretation
The impetuosity and boundless energy of youth; energy and aspiration without direction; a provider of force; faithful friend and associate unable to take control of a situation; brilliant and daring energies; adolescent enthusiasm. Reversed: Denying free spirit; indecision and instability; evil news.

Knight of Wands – Flexible Intuition

Astride a galloping battle horse the extremely confident Knight of Wands charges towards his goal, passing pyramids in the distance. His tunic is decorated with elemental salamanders of fire and gold and red flames decorate his robe and helmet.

Interpretation
Exciting youngsters in your life; sudden changes in life direction; expressing new and exciting philosophical and religious perceptions; intuitive messages from spiritual domains lead to a journey; adventures in consciousness; passionate creativity; flight and precipitate action. Reversed: Disappearing without trace; loss of inspiration; psychological cul-de-sacs requiring forceful change.

Queen of Wands – Initiatory Self

Upon her throne of fire, decorated with lions and holding an open sunflower, the Queen of Wands faces the south, from which the sun's rays are strongest and most penetrating. The pyramids behind her and the cat at her feet symbolize the Egyptian heritage of her divine right.

Interpretation
A dark, chaste and honorable woman facing life issues; Aries or fire sign people, especially women. Sureness and penetration of the open self; powerful self-assertion and awareness of direction; success in business and creative affairs. Reversed: Lack of self-awareness or self-assertion; obstinacy and jealousy; experiencing opposition to your pure energy.

King of Wands – Conscious Self
Wearing a flowing cape, a crown of flames and a leonine medallion, the King of Wands sits upon a throne emblazoned with lions. At his feet is a salamander, the alchemical symbol for fire. He gazes towards the East where his totem the Sun rises to bring light into the day.

Interpretation
A dark, honest and friendly man; Leo or fire sign people; the lion within. Self-consciousness and commitment to the quest of attaining greater awareness; spiritual vision and the need to be fixed upon the right path; loyalty and faithfulness. Reversed: Stubbornness from fixed views incapable of change; spiritual arrogance.

THE SUIT OF CUPS

Cups are the element water and the psychological function of feeling.

Ace of Cups – True Heart
A hand from the clouds surrounded by dew holds a cup from which four streams of water fall into a tranquil pond. A white dove descends to place a cross-marked wafer into the cup.

Interpretation
The open heart is true at the beginning of the spiritual adventure; joy and contentment; abundance and fertility;

The Cups Cards

expressing true feelings; openness to deep feelings; the regeneration of love. Reversed: Inability to open the heart; false heart; instability; emotional inconstancy and insensitivity.

Two of Cups – Love
A young woman and man are exchanging cups to pledge their union. Above them a caduceus of Hermes is crowned by a lion's head.

Interpretation
The interrelationship between male and female energies within; nurturing and inspired love; sympathy and concord; clarity and focus in relationship. Reversed: Lack of nurturing; inappropriate feelings between the sexes; too much dependency.

Three of Cups – Abundance
Three maidens lofting cups toast themselves and the bountiful world around them.

Interpretation
Expressing emotional diversity and plenty brings abundance in the outer world; expressive relationships with equals; victory; healing energies from a group or family; deep communication and communion with others. Reversed: Trapped emotions and buried feelings; inexpressive relationships; emotional breakdown; excessive pleasures; achievement.

Four of Cups – Blended Pleasure
A young man seated under a tree contemplates three cups before him and one held by a hand emerging from a cloud. He looks withdrawn and unhappy.

Interpretation
Deep sensitivity to outer influences brings a need for withdrawal; devotion to higher feelings; emotional over-expression;

succumbing to seduction and pleasure; being confused by outer/inner emotional conflicts. Reversed: New instructions and teachers; clouded reality from taking in more than one can understand; disappointment with luxury.

Five of Cups – Emotional Disappointment
A dark, cloaked figure looks down at three spilt cups with two upright cups behind him. The bridge over the river in the background leads to a small isolated castle.

Interpretation
Deep disappointment despite fullness; courage and work required in a relationship; relationships which do not correspond to expectations; unsatisfactory inheritance; a bitter marriage; strong unconscious needs not met. Reversed: Upsetting news; new alliances with old friends; projects with unknown values and uncertain goals.

Six of Cups – Nostalgia
Two young children play in a garden with cups filled with blossoming flowers.

Interpretation
Memories of blissful childhood times bring pleasure and happiness; positive reinforcement from past memories; contact and identification with the inner child; receiving supportive or parental feelings. Reversed: Renewal; the potential for regeneration; emotional turmoil.

Seven of Cups – Sentiment
A dark figure observes cups filled with fantastic visionary treasures in the clouds.

Interpretation
Reflections or projections of emotional states upon the ideal; attaining the insubstantial; sentimental attachments; need to balance psychic sensitivity with honesty. Reversed: False emotional projections; being overwhelmed by desire or taken in by fantasy; projects based on will.

Eight of Cups – Abandonment
A dejected man walks away from a pyramid of cups towards the mountains and the sea. The full moon gleams above.

Interpretation
Abandoning one's previous feelings; retreat after being emotionally drained; the decline of a formerly fulfilling relationship; departing from family; timidity and mildness. Reversed: Joy and happiness; returning to face difficult emotional pressures; the end of isolation.

Nine of Cups – Satisfaction
An overweight man with crossed arms sits in front of a table full of wine goblets, implying plenty and abundance.

Interpretation
An awareness of emotional satisfaction; material security leads to feeling secure; concord; satisfaction in an outstanding issue. Reversed: Truth and loyalty; psychological vulnerability; openness to emotional pressure.

Ten of Cups – Contentment
A vivid rainbow of cups arch over an ecstatic couple and their dancing children. Beyond is a beautiful homeland beyond the river.

Interpretation
Emotional completion; discovering the riches in your dreams; heartfelt repose: successful artistic activity; idealistic feelings must be experienced in reality. Reversed: False security; dreams exceed reality; indignation and egocentricity.

Page of Cups – Pure Feeling
A fair and attractive page contemplates a fish arising from his cup. Behind him the waters rise and fall.

Interpretation
An emotionally involved partner; studying feelings as they arise; turning fish into princesses; fantasies about potential

openings; the beginning of a relationship; meditation and study. Reversed: Emotional detachment; dreaming about fantastic relationships; emotional dependency.

Knight of Cups – Graceful Feeling
A beautiful and gentle knight wearing a winged helmet holds a cup towards his future as he dreams of true love.

Interpretation
Approaching the emotional core of one's being; significant dreams; passive and graceful responses to emotional situations; fateful and destined relationship in mind; messengers; an advance or proposition or invitation. Reversed: Evasive emotions; false ideals; subtle tricks; duplicity.

Queen of Cups – Emotional Integrity
In a seashell throne surrounded by water, a beauty like Aphrodite gazes at a magical cup and sees her dreams within.

Interpretation
Emotional service and nurturing comes from an unexpected source; actions inspired by dreamy feelings; devotion and happiness; enjoyment of giving support to a partner; wisdom and virtue. Reversed: A distinguished woman not to be trusted; perversity and treachery.

King of Cups – Unconditional Love
A stable and severe king sits on his seashell throne in the sea, holding a cup and sceptre. A ship passes on one side and a dolphin on the other. He wears a fish dangling from his neck and is at home in the waves.

Interpretation
A fair and emotionally secure person; emotional commitment and unconditional love; an emotional obligation is fulfilled; scientists and artists unite; creative intelligence. Reversed: Emotional insecurity and lack of commitment; injustice; scandals due to uncontrolled feelings; losses through passion.

THE SUIT OF SWORDS

Swords are the element air and the psychological function of thinking.

Ace of Swords – Innovative Thought
A hand coming from a cloud holds a sword penetrating a crown draped with laurel leaves.

Interpretation
Communicating ideas for their own sake; invention and discrimination in thought; placing priority upon ideas; mental identification. Reversed: Detachment and abstraction; a breakdown of communication; a lack of ideas or goals; difficulties with intimacy.

Two of Swords – Balance
A blindfolded woman sits by the sea balancing two crossed swords on her shoulders. A waxing moon sits over her left shoulder.

Interpretation
Conforming with others' ideas; relationships with similarity of ideas and goals; meditative mind balancing choices; affection and intimacy; friendship in arms. Reversed: False ideas about others; projection; disloyalty.

Three of Swords – Sorrow
Three swords pierce a heart amidst rain clouds.

Interpretation
Being influenced by past difficulties; sadness removing you from present time; difficulties in relationships due to disloyalty; delay. Reversed: Clearing up past attitudes; investigating negative thoughts about your past.

Four of Swords – Peace
The tomb of a knight lying in state with three swords on the wall and one on his tomb.

The Swords Cards

Interpretation
Allowing destructive ideas to pass away; remembering life as sacred; exile from society; resolving conflicts through unattachment. Reversed: Obsession with negative past influences; denying yourself rest; wise administration; economy and caution in all matters.

Five of Swords – Defeat
A man carrying three swords has just vanquished two foes in battle. He possesses the field as they walk away in defeat.

Interpretation
The defeat and destruction of a negative behaviour pattern; lack of integration of subpersonalities; destruction of existing ideas; loss and dishonour. Reversed: Unreliability because of unpredictable ideas; not accepting obsolete ideas.

Six of Swords – Progressive Mind
A ferryman punts two hooded passengers across a river. Six vertical swords stand in the front of the boat.

Interpretation
Progressive ideas require unusual means of communication; integrating ideas; separation due to inventiveness; eccentricity of thought; a journey by water; acting as an emissary. Reversed: Ideas not accepted as being too inventive; lack of originality; confessions.

Seven of Swords – Futility
Before a tournament tent a man carries off five swords, but leaves two behind in the ground.

Interpretation
Taking on too many new ideas; unconventional and individual attitudes provoke ostracism; plans that may fail; unrealistic designs; competition without resolution. Reversed: Eccentric attitudes; good advice and counsel; instructing others; uncertainty.

Eight of Swords – Interference
A bound and masked woman stands amidst a field of swords.

Interpretation
Being trapped by obsolete ideas or mental concepts; blindness to one's own communications; overly analytical; mental originality without proper focussing. Reversed: Disquiet; being trapped by design; opposition; unforeseen difficulties; too much complexity.

Nine of Swords – Deception
A weeping woman sits up in her bed decorated with zodiacal symbols, underneath a wall of horizontal swords.

Interpretation
Desolation caused by negative thinking; failure of a plan of action; disappointment from excessive criticism of the self. Reversed: Being trapped in negative thought patterns; suspicion caused within oneself; fears supported by others; inconsistent ideas.

Ten of Swords – Ruin
A prostrate figure is pierced by ten swords.

Interpretation
Afflicted by negative ideas; the death of a concept or life direction; contradictory information kills communication; lies and sadness. Reversed: Advantages and profit; the breakdown of authority.

Page of Swords – Pure Thinking
A figure ready for action holds an upright sword amidst rough countryside.

Interpretation
Bringing ideas into the physical world; mental identification; the need to examine thoughts; logic and organizational enterprises; secrecy and hidden communications. Reversed: Resistance to thinking; being unaware of your ideas; the unforeseen; sickness.

Knight of Swords – Creative Thinking
A romantic hero charges, scattering his enemies before him.

Interpretation
Inspiration that is not bound by any constructs; free-ranging mind; cleverness and skill at self-expression and communication; verbal jousting and competition; changes and versatility. Reversed: Constrained by attitude; limited intelligence; superficial ideas and skills; shallow thought.

Queen of Swords – Perceptive Thinking
A regal woman raises a vertical sword and extends her left hand in a gesture of acknowledgment.

Interpretation
Balanced feminine thinking and communication; integration of thoughts and personality; a peacemaker or mediator; partnership with others and the world; chastity. Reversed: Psychological imbalance weighted toward the feminine; a vindictive woman; feelings of malice.

King of Swords – Judgmental Thinking
A stern ruler sits in judgment holding a sword of discrimination vertically.

Interpretation
The discriminative male principle; balanced masculine thinking and judgment; an arbitrator or advocate; power and command of the mind; authority; strategic thinking. Reversed: Lacking discrimination with blatant favouritism; imbalanced male thinking; judgmental attitudes; cruelty and perversity.

THE SUIT OF PENTACLES

Pentacles are the element earth and the psychological function of sensation.

Ace of Pentacles – Contentment
A hand extending from the clouds holds a pentacle above a beautiful enclosed garden.

The Pentacles Cards

95

Interpretation
Balance between body and higher functions of mind, spirit and feelings; ecstasy; inheritance of earthly power and possessions; good health and abundance. Reversed: Imbalance between higher functions and physical reality; illness; abandoning or losing possessions.

Two of Pentacles – Change
A dancing young man holds pentacles in each hand, joined by an endless cord making a lemniscate, symbol of infinity.

Interpretation
Understanding cycles of birth, death and rebirth in the physical world; expanding awareness through change; recognizing the idea of polarity in life; agitation and duality. Reversed: Anxiety caused by limited views; being trapped on the wheel of rebirth; life as a grind; futility and simulated enjoyment.

Three of Pentacles – Skilful Action
A mason or sculptor rebuilds an archway in sight of two monks.

Interpretation
Understanding artistic priorities in creating a bridge of understanding; taking control of a project or stage of development; rebuilding the structure; mobility and aristocracy. Reversed: Purely mechanical actions; allowing bridges to break down; indolence and pettiness; weakness.

Four of Pentacles – Power
A crowned man wearing a pentacle crown rotates a pentacle in his arms and stands on two more against the background of a large city.

Interpretation
Awareness of boundaries brings power and possessions; practical and realistic methods for attaining physical security; defining oneself by possessions or wealth; thinking about the real world. Reversed: Possessiveness; unclear boundaries; inability to limit oneself.

Five of Pentacles – Poverty
Two injured and poor people pass under a stained-glass window during a snowstorm.

Interpretation
Material insecurity caused by misunderstanding the physical world; unusual priorities; abusing or ignoring the body; letting go of worry about financial matters; release. Reversed: Disorder and chaos from abandoning the world order; breakdown of physical structures; strain, discord and ruin.

Six of Pentacles – Success
A successful, rich and sensitive merchant bestows money on the poor and needy.

Interpretation
Harmonious representation of the earthly element; positive sensations, gifts and gratification; present prosperity and success in worldly affairs, but eventual change. Reversed: Desire and materialistic attitudes; physical changes requiring penitence.

Seven of Pentacles – Anxiety
A worried young man leans on his staff and observes the fruits of his labour.

Interpretation
Fear of satisfaction or completion; limitations in productivity; recognizing barriers; the need for exchange; the harvest means the end of a project or endeavour. Reversed: Inability to complete; resistance to physical requirements; anxiety regarding financial commitments.

Eight of Pentacles – Craft
An artist carves pentacles for trophies.

Interpretation
Attending to details in one's work or creative efforts; skill in material matters; successful planning for the future; knowledge

of the workings of the world. Reversed: Avoiding the details; material ignorance; difficulties in saving.

Nine of Pentacles – Accomplishment
A beautiful woman with a hunting falcon on her wrist stands amidst a splendid garden of great abundance.

Interpretation
Awareness of realistic goals; bringing desires and needs into line; adjusting goals to allow satisfaction; good luck and good management. Reversed: Unrealistic expectations in the physical world; being governed by base instincts; bad faith.

Ten of Pentacles – Wealth
A woman and man accompanied by their child converse beneath an archway leading to a manor house. Two white dogs look curiously at an old man in front of the doorway.

Interpretation
Protecting the security of the family and home; the family system of generations; a loving environment; a final abode. Reversed: Breakdown of the family system; lack of understanding between generations; misusing past memories.

Page of Pentacles – Pure Form
A youthful gentleman meditates on the pentacle he is holding in his raised hands, ignoring the countryside around him. A sacred grove awaits him on a distant hillside.

Interpretation
The stage just before transformation; meditation on strength and beauty; approaching spiritual work; application and studying; reflection upon material and spiritual goals. Reversed: Resisting transformation; being unable to detach and obtain objectivity; dissipating spiritual possibilities; unfavourable news.

Knight of Pentacles – Created Form
A solid and secure horseman holds a pentacle, but looks beyond it to the distant horizon.

Interpretation
Great energy applied to basic and solid tasks; long-term expectations and goals; attention to physical details; responsibility and service as a profession. Reversed: Lack of inspiration; inability to deal with present situations; too much emphasis upon stability.

Queen of Pentacles – Nurturing Form
A dark and introspective woman protects the pentacle she holds on her lap. Her throne stands amidst a wonderful arbour as she meditates upon the plight of the soul.

Interpretation
Searching for the inner meaning of the physical world; correcting priorities; feminine intelligence and introspection; a great soul; seeing all elements within the physical. Reversed: Suspicion caused by materialism; ambition and detachment.

King of Pentacles – Skilful Form
A dark man sits upon a throne decorated with bulls' heads in great solidity and security. Behind the throne a prosperous city stands.

Interpretation
Manifesting skill in the physical world; the ability to build and sustain; realizing intelligence; aptitude for business and attainments in the material sphere; fixed concerns. Reversed: Victimized by materialism; being arrogant due to wealth; being trapped by physical trappings.

THE MAGICIAN.

6 · THE TAROT READING

Reading the tarot cards is divination, a ritual or ceremonial act, a magical action and a meditation. Whether the function of the reading is as part of a therapeutic process or as a way to understand past, present or future trends does not affect this basic mechanism of the tarot.

Divination means 'from the divine', and implies that communication with higher intelligence or beings is sought, although within the psychological context this may be understood as higher aspects of one's self, higher levels of consciousness or positive subpersonalities. A question is posed and the answer determined by interpreting patterns created in the natural world or by a personal and conscious act as in the case of laying out tarot cards. In ancient times divination took a multitude of forms, especially in cultures which lived in nature and communed with the forces of the world which they called their gods and goddesses, and also contacted the spirits which lay within or beyond their goddesses and gods.

The movement of birds across the sky, the form and colour of the entrails of animals, the patterns of bones or stones thrown onto the ground, the numbers of groups of sticks or stalks divided and counted, or the drawing of images upon stones, bones or cards were the raw material of these mantic arts. In each case a vocabulary of symbolic patterns or shapes determined an answer to the question. The diviner interpreted the oracular response and, as such, became a direct conduit, or what today would be called a channel, to the gods or goddesses. It was the function of such persons to guide the destiny of the soul, the individual, the tribe or even the nation. Indeed these oracular acts were taken as directly inspired by the divinity. We can look back to history and find the importance of oracular centres such as Delphi, Thebes, Glastonbury, Tara, Babylon, Sidon and others spread across Europe and Asia. In virtually all cultures such contact with the divine was encouraged as a central belief, if not the core of religious observance. If one did not consult the god or goddess, how could one discover the correct path? Today we seek the gods or goddesses within ourselves.

The mantic art creates a field within which images may appear which are keys to current, but also past and future states, both in the interior, spiritual or mental world and their corresponding effects in the outer physical world. In an ancient Roman oracle which read the flights of birds, the querent (questioner) would define an area of open sky in his line of sight, which may be a square or a circle. Once the oracular meditation begins, whatever enters this mentally-defined space is a significant symbol. The reader determines certain conventions, which may be personal or may be universal, and evaluates all input based upon these 'laws'. For example, it may be that the left is the past and the right the future, the bottom unknown influences emerging from the earth, and above influences coming down from spiritual sources. Given this scheme, if a large grey rain cloud enters the left side and passes gradually across the field to exit on the right, it could mean that a time of ignorance and incorrect thoughts (the grey cloud) coming from past perceptions (the left) gradually obscures the central issues (the centre of the field) until they pass by of their own volition into the future. If the object entering were a majestic eagle from above, it could indicate a divine revelation inspiring great courage. In time a complete system was created through which accurate symbols could be discovered and interpreted.

In our time of psychiatry, group therapy, psychotherapy, alternative healing, shamanism, ritual magic, Eastern religion and religious fundamentalism, the principle of the oracle mirrors have returned into prominence as a way to the true Self. We have collectively lost our souls and are trying to return to the centre by experimenting with the I Ching, Tarot, the Nordic Runes and others. Within this context, the tarot is a primary tool of self-awareness.

But how do oracles work? The psychologist Carl Jung studied these phenomena for many decades and indeed wrote a famous foreword to the translation of the I Ching by Richard Wilhelm. Jung postulated that there is a 'synchronicity' between outer events and inner psychic states, which means that outer and inner influences are linked by similar meaning, and that there is no such thing as coincidence. Every event in the universe is connected in some way with every other event, if only the connection can be known. Any technique for tapping into the temporal flow, whether it be yarrow stalks in the I Ching or tarot cards, allows access to this fount of information and understanding. The relationship of thought to reality described by Jung is a view held in the East for millennia and is only recently being accepted as an aspect of reality by the most progressive modern physicists.

Tarot taps into the information available in the space-time continuum at a specific time and place. The symbols of the tarot are the receivers, as it were, which respond to these unique qualities. They are mirrors of the self of the querent, both in the sense that they reflect the state of awareness of certain issues, and that they provide many layers of meaning which will be decoded according to the openness and symbol-reading abilities of the querent.

THE QUESTION AND THE QUESTIONER

The tarot process begins with a thought initiating the reading itself. In some ways this first impulse is the essence of the reading itself. If only we could remember and understand our precise motivations in asking a question about life, we might discover the answer then and there. As this is rarely possible, great importance must be placed upon the formulation of the question.

While in our first contact with tarot we are likely to be the querent and nominate someone else to be the reader or interpreter of the cards, it must be understood that the ultimate goal is to be both querent and reader. When understanding increases and self-awareness blossoms, it becomes clear that the entire process takes place within the psyche. Seen from this perspective, all outer events, whether they be physical, emotional, mental or spiritual, are simply reflections of our pure being in the world, ways by which we work through our karma – our attachment to previous patterns of being and action, and vehicles through which we may develop a higher means of awareness. We could say that the function of the process is to make our intimations of the world or ourselves more explicit, to take what is forming and describe it, to eliminate the differences between ourselves and the world within which we live out our destiny. Therefore, from the duality of querent and reader comes a third, higher viewpoint which will reconcile the opposites and describe a path to unity.

The practice of tarot brings the realization that if the true nature of the question were understood, that itself would constitute the answer. In practice, the way in which a question is asked often betrays the answer, as though the answer is in some mysterious way hidden within the question. Similarly, using tarot makes us aware that the answers lie within the images, simply awaiting our recognition of them, like our future soul mate in a gigantic, magical ballroom.

The formulation of the question has the primary function of focusing the mind upon the self and its true issues. It is often the case that the more precise the question, the more preordained the answer. Often those people who apparently require precise answers ask vague questions, implying that they are unsure what the question really is. It is therefore an axiom that the quality of the question is directly related to the quality of the answer. When a question is clearly expressed, the answer is usually not far away. Since the objective of the process is to link these two issues, understanding the interrelationship between these two worlds can bring great understanding.

When a question involves another person or outer circumstances apparently beyond the querent's control, one must immediately recognize that an issue of projection is central to the answer. Why is the outside world affecting this person in such a complete way? A request for a more tightly formulated question will often give rise to resistances and breakthroughs which will initiate an inward-looking process. The inclusion of the querent brings the question to life. The more personal the question, the closer to home the entire process.

A valuable exercise is to ask yourself to formulate a question which is critical to you right now. As you try to formulate the question, feel and observe what goes on inside, what territory your mind covers on its way to discovering the question. Often you will review possible answers while formulating the questions, or experience blocks to asking certain ones. In a tarot reading, the chances are that the cards will symbolize this process.

In some situations, the querent does not have a specific question. The litany of many first-time tarot querents is: 'What is going to happen to me in the future?' In this case the mere act of contemplating possible questions will at least focus the mind and concentrate the attention upon the present time.

THE RITUAL OF TAROT

The tarot reading is a powerful interaction between the reader and the querent. In learning to interpret the tarot cards there are some important mechanisms which it is a good idea to reflect upon.

The primary objective of the preliminaries to the ritual of tarot is to allow the querent and reader to relax, to quieten the mind and to concentrate upon the issues at hand. If the process is to be important for you, it is recommended to follow some or all of the following guidelines. You can choose those you feel comfortable with and those which prove to function in a satisfactory way.

1. Create as controlled an environment as you can, including determining the time of day when your concentration will

be best and you are least likely to be disturbed. It may be important to choose a phase of the moon which is sympathetic to the action: full moons bring conflicts and dualities into the open, whereas the new moon is better for exploring deep unconscious influences and more hidden issues. The time of day is also important. It is often more effective to do tarot readings after sunset or at night, when the natural energies are at their most still.

2. Many tarot readers find a silk cloth to wrap around their deck or a box in which to place the cards when they are not being used. The energy of the cards should not be diluted by contact with others or with impure surroundings; silk is thought to insulate them. Often it is desirable to isolate the cards somewhere where they are unlikely to be disturbed or seen by others. It is also useful to have a sheet of silk or cloth upon which to do the reading.

3. Turn out the light. Light some candles. Burn incense.

4. Wear comfortable and loose clothing which is sympathetic to the exercise, possibly a robe or gown. It may also be desirable to meditate before approaching the cards.

5. Recite an invocation or one of the affirmations to create the correct atmosphere for the reading, especially if there is an intention to generate a particular energy or effect through the ritual. You may want to have ritual elements available: a cup of wine, a sword, a wand and a pentacle or coin — options which can intensify the mood.

6. It is important that the two individuals involved in the process are psychically linked and to create bridges by which this can be achieved. Both must participate in the magic of the enterprise for its power to be released. Make eye contact, attempt to join energies in the process ahead.

7. It is valuable to keep a diary or book in which to write tarot readings, the questions, the querents, the significant cards if not the entire reading. Record the time and place, the atmosphere and other details which bring the event to life. You will enjoy and learn about tarot by keeping such records. It is also an important gauge to determine how you are progressing in the process of becoming a tarot practitioner.

THE LAYOUT OF THE CARDS

While the following chapter details some of the more common spreads for the cards, it is also important how you lay the cards out on the table. It is a ritualistic process, an invocation to the powers, and an opening of the unconscious energies of both participants which can be encouraged by the correct laying out of the cards.

8. Let the querent hold the cards before the process begins. It is essential to be comfortable and to realize that energy must be transmitted to the cards in order for the process to work at maximum efficiency. Let daily stresses and cares wash away, and concentrate on stilling both your mind and the querent's. Have the querent take a few minutes and meditate on the question, and then, while shuffling the cards, have 'him' formulate in 'his' own mind the exact question or questions 'he' will ask. Gather your mental and intuitive powers and begin the procedure.

9. When the querent is ready with a question, have 'him' lay the deck face down on the table and prepare to cut the cards. This cutting process acts like the sword of discrimination. The deck should be cut approximately in half and put together again. The process can be repeated twice more for a proper triple cut. The deck is now ready for the process of the reading.

    Each card will be taken from the top of the deck in turn and laid out in the same way. Whether they are turned from top to bottom, or from right to left, just ensure that you turn them the same way each time. If the first card is reversed, turn the entire deck around and continue placing the cards.

    Many tarot commentators state that when a card is reversed (upside down) in the spread, it represents the negative of the quality or information symbolized by the card. A more balanced way to utilize reversed cards is to accept that the reversed cards represent shadow qualities – qualities which the individual

Upright   Reversed

Figure 4

possesses but does not identify with, or projects onto others or the world. It is natural that upright cards are qualities of which the individual is conscious, and it is only appropriate that the reversed cards identify aspects of the individual which remain unconscious. A reading where a majority of the cards are reversed would imply a high degree of unconsciousness in the querent. Some commentators, such as Crowley, do not use the reverse qualities and read each card as though it were upright.

Eventually you will discover a way to present the cards which feels right to you and your querents.

THE MAGICIAN.

7 · TAROT SPREADS

While this chapter deals primarily with some spreads to be used for tarot readings, it is also appropriate to introduce a technique for learning about the tarot.

A primary obstacle to using tarot is to become familiar with all of the cards in the tarot deck. While their images are quite familiar to many people, it is essential to create a technique for bringing about deeper knowledge and understanding of the cards and their wisdom. Naturally it is desirable to be familiar enough with the cards to know their meanings, but this may take some time and quite a bit of application. Rather than learning their meanings by rote, it is often better to try to understand the language of the symbols so that you can reconstruct and reinvent the meanings each time you use the cards. Like interpreting dreams, it is more important that you learn to develop an ability to freely associate with the cards than it is to 'know' their literal meanings, which in any event are far from agreed.

THE DAILY CARD

One of the best ways to learn the tarot is to first take the twenty-two major arcana cards, isolate them from the rest of the deck, and place them in an important position in your bedroom or study, where you can see them every day, particularly at the beginning and end of the day. **The**

Daily Card Spread technique involves choosing a card every morning as a device for seeing how the qualities of the card will come into being throughout the day. When you rise, shuffle the cards, cut them, and when you have placed them down on a table, turn over the top card, which will be your **Significator**, the card for the day. The significator is also the term for the central card in a tarot spread which refers to the querent, which is you in this case.

Look at the card, and try and find one or more symbols which inspire you or take your fancy. See the colours and textures represented on the card, and try to enhance their reality in your mind (see page 133 for more information on visualization techniques). Allow the environment of the card to permeate you, to become part of you, or you a part of it. Sometimes you will express the card's meaning yourself, while many times they will be acted out by others around you. This may correlate with whether the card is upright or reversed. Try to work out if there is such a correlation, whether overt or obtuse. If you feel a resistance to the images or personifications or actions on the cards, try to understand what you are resisting, and why. If the card bores you or makes you uneasy, explore those feelings and the questions and situations which bring them up.

Feel what it must be like to be the individual represented on the card. Put yourself in their place, whether female or male, adult or child, and imagine being that person or expressing that quality in yourself. In the case of animal representations, identify with the animal within yourself.

When you have exhausted the images in the card and are confident that you have experienced it fully, look in this book and read the text associated with the card. Read the *Guided Imagery* and allow it to sink in, and open yourself up to the journey it describes. When you have finished, read the *Affirmation*, and if you cannot learn it on the spot, write it down on a slip of paper and repeat it throughout the day.

Think of the card's qualities as a part of you throughout the day. When you draw the Fool, go through a day where you allow yourself to be young again, be naive, take chances, or explore areas to which you never usually give attention. Try to understand why the card pictures the scene it does and how it could be relevant to you.

At the end of the day, review what has happened throughout the day. Which part of you was dominant, which part was passive? Did you feel integrated or fragmented? Was the card a useful guide or a straitjacket? Was your intuition more prominent than usual? Did you respect your inner attitudes? All these questions and their answers are valuable feedback not only for your process of learning the cards, but also your own psychological development.

In this way you will not only begin to learn about the cards, but you will understand how to identify with them. You will see how your moods and those of people around you seem to correspond to the card you have drawn. Some days the identification will be stronger and more powerful than other days, but that is characteristic of the way we function.

THE CHALLENGE OF THE CROSSING CARD

After you have become familiar with the major arcana cards, you may want to include the court cards and the minor arcana in your Daily Card reading. This provides you with three layers of meaning. The major arcana are archetypal qualities you express, the court cards are people or personality types you are likely to meet or express in yourself, and the minor arcana are actions and interactions which may or may not have archetypal significance. Some days will be critical and others will be transitional, just as we would expect.

In traditional tarot lore, the central card in a reading functions like the Daily Card as a focus of the question, as a significator of the querent or the present time, and as the potential catalyst for the issue or issues contained in the question. It is the starting point and also the answer to the question, simultaneously. This implies that the answer lies within the question, similarly to the way in which the resolution of any psychological issue lies within the individual psyche. To project the answer outside yourself is to project it rather than own it.

The **Crossing** is placed across the significator or central card and symbolizes the challenge to the question and querent. It symbolizes the energy which blocks the principle shown by the significator, and simultaneously shows the bridge over which the querent must pass in order to resolve the issue and achieve wholeness. This is one reason why each of the major arcana cards may be understood as having both conscious and unconscious interpretations. The unconscious is usually associated with the negative because of its identity with the shadow, which has always been seen as being mysterious, threatening and destructive. We fear and avoid our own negative sides, yet integration requires probing these depths, bringing its contents up into consciousness, and utilizing them as necessary parts of our whole being. This is why the crossing card has such power and importance, and why virtually all tarot spreads utilize this combination of two cards in its centre. We need to explore the crossing card in greater detail and with more insight than the other cards, particularly if it is reversed. In a way, all other cards represent a fragmentation of the central issue of self and shadow.

Figure 5 Card Crossing the Significator

111

THE ORIENTATION OF THE CARDS

Even traditional tarot spreads may be seen to utilize a common symbolic orientation. The symbolism of orientations was initially used in early mantic arts which involved the flights of birds or the positions of stones thrown on the ground, and were later rediscovered by Carl Jung in analysing his patients' paintings. When one understands this language it becomes possible to look at anything and discover its hidden meaning.

The issue is one of boundaries. In the unconsciousness of early childhood, there are no boundaries between our emerging self and the world around us. Our mother, for example, is often seen as an extension of us. But as we develop through childhood we gradually realize that we have a self, delimited by our body, and the not-self, which is the rest of the world around us. The creation of this initial boundary is one of the first acts in life. We could say that consciousness is a sophistication of this early, initial boundary we create between ourselves and the world. The object of meditation, religious practices, psychotherapy and mantic arts such as tarot is to re-establish the unity which preceded the boundaries which we created to define ourselves, and which separated us from the world.

The orientation follows the compass points (N,E,S,W) and the angles of the astrological horoscope (Ascendant/Descendant, Midheaven/Immum Coeli), all of which are divisions of the circle by four. These fourfold qualities appear in art, architecture, dreams, mandalas and other visual areas, and although the primary way of understanding them is astrological, as Jung pointed out it is also archetypal.

The first division is around the horizontal axis (or the horizon). Below the horizon is the realm of the unconscious, the underworld, the shadow and the unknown. This domain is subjective, indirect and comes from within. Above the horizon is the realm of consciousness, the higher world, the visible and the known. This domain is objective, direct and comes from without or above. In a tarot reading, cards in the lower half signify qualities which are emerging from the unconscious of

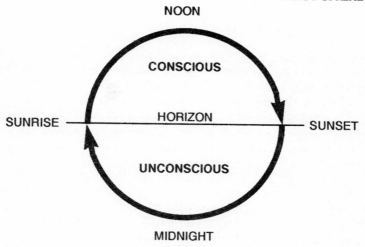

Figure 6   *The Horizontal Axis*

the querent, while cards in the upper half signify qualities which are emerging from the consciousness of the querent.

The second division is around the vertical axis (see Figure 7). To the left, the place of the rising sun, is the realm of the self, the personality, the body and one's own domain. To the right, the place of the setting sun, is the realm of the not-self, one's partners and partnerships, one's relationship with the outer world. The left side is us, the right is them. The function of the left side is to learn to own the qualities which are parts of the self, such as how we act, what we look like, how we see ourselves and how well we understand who we are. In contrast, the right half shows what we project onto others or the outside world, how we make relationships and whom we attract, how others see us and how we allow their interpretations of us.

We superimpose the two axes to make a cross, the symbolic cross upon which Christ was crucified and which we accept as defining qualities in our life on earth in a physical body. The four quadrants symbolize aspects of us which are ideally in balance, although in reality there is always a tension between them and different values placed upon them. We tend to

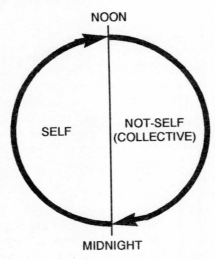

Figure 7   The Vertical Axis

overvalue one axis and undervalue the other. For example, if we orient ourself towards a public life where others' perceptions of us are of primary importance (the right half), then we often sacrifice the secure sense of self characteristic of those who value the left half most highly. When there is such a difference across these axes, psychologically the undervalued functions are often expressed as the shadow of the overvalued function. Thus the immaculate public figure has a shady and murky personal life, as we have seen in the British royal family. Understanding these crosses in our life is a primary function in tarot.

INTERPRETATION AND SYMBOLISM IN THE READING

A question of primary importance in doing a tarot reading for yourself or others is: How does one arrive at accurate conclusions from the cards? The answer is, predictably, quite complex. If you look to the popular source books about the tarot you will find mention of the actual process of arriving at an interpretation of the cards missing. This may be because it is not easy to explain.

The issues at stake in converting a card in a tarot spread to a sensible interpretation which can be understood by a client are many. What is obvious is that the interpretation must be a combination of (a) the traditional interpretive meanings of the cards, (b) images or ideas derived from the symbols on the cards, and (c) a feeling or intuitive response to the individual and her or his question. The interpretive meanings given in this book are intended only as a guide to possible directions implied by each card, rather than literal interpretations, but beginners may be tempted to look at the card in a spread, turn to the appropriate page of this or other books, and read the interpretation which seems most relevant to the client. With experience and practice, a tarot reader will learn and remember the meanings associated with each card and store this information for easy access. But, an encyclopaedic memory of traditional interpretations will not make one a superior tarot reader. This requires the use of intuition, feeling and compassion for the client and his or her plight, and the ability to derive from the symbols upon the cards the higher meanings needed.

The interpretation of the symbols on tarot cards is a process similar to interpreting dreams. In both cases the images must be seen as metaphors for unconscious principles of the dreamer/client. The personae of the cards are aspects of the client's personality, their environments are moods or attitudes of the client, the symbols of the cards are psychic mechanisms or tools which the individual may choose to use. Thus the sword sticking into a prone body can be seen as an important idea (swords are the thinking process and ideas) penetrating an individual who has given up hope (the prone position). Trees will imply the growth of whatever they protect and, if in the distance, show that there is growth in the future. Warriors indicate the need to act, beautiful women the need to be aware of appearances, children the necessity of acknowledging the child within.

As in dream interpretation, it is not necessary to interpret every symbol on every card, but to meditate upon the cards and talk about what you happen to focus upon. It is natural to see a card one way today, and very differently tomorrow. In every situation the appropriate images will 'pop out' at you. The more you trust your intuition and try to put yourself in the place of your client, the more accurate and appropriate the images which present themselves will be.

As in dreams, there may not be an obvious time sequence, but rather a jumble of images apparently thrown together at random. One of your tasks is to take the multitude of images and apply a sequence to them. This process may be obvious. The Fool followed by Judgement would imply naivety leading to the necessity to make a choice, while the other way around would show that choices lead to naive actions. It is said that dream images have no sequence when they are dreamed, but that our conscious mind imposes a structure upon them at the instant we awake. In tarot interpretation we intend to do the same thing.

The position of the card should influence the way you interpret it. For cards in 'conscious' positions at the top of a spread for example, be as conscious as you can in rationally finding a meaning for the cards, while for cards in 'unconscious' positions at the bottom of a spread, be as free and unstructured as possible in intuitively deriving an appropriate meaning. In time you will learn to allow your mind, feelings and intuition to work together, and to blend these seemingly different functions together in a coherent whole.

The client also participates in the reading by their presence. Look at them closely as they enter the room, sit down, listen to you, take the cards, shuffle them and respond to the interpretation. Watch for clues about where they are and search especially for unconscious signals they may be sending out. Their resistance to certain cards will show you the cards represent important principles which they are blocking. If they project qualities onto their partners, friends or on you, these qualities have been difficult to integrate and need to be identified and followed up by you. Pay attention to the images they relate to or don't relate to, notice their changing posture and attention throughout the consultation. The more clues you have to work with, the more full and complete the atmosphere and the more accurate the reading.

Compare the interpretations given in the book with your own intuitively derived ideas, and modify them by the position of the card. Mention when unconscious and disjointed images fall in places which should be rational and conscious These displacements are critical. With practice, the dedication to learn the key words, and the willingness to act and talk about feelings and intuitions, you will be able to provide stimulating, challenging and accurate interpretations to your friends and clients.

The spreads that follow are a combination of traditional spreads and original spreads which utilize the symbolic qualities presented earlier.

THE PAST-PRESENT-FUTURE SPREAD

One of the most effective of the simpler spreads is the Past-Present-Future Spread utilizing four cards. The sequence in which the cards are laid down is:

1. The Significator (Present Time)
2. The Crossing (challenges Present) – laid across the Significator
3. The Past – laid to the left of the Significator and Crossing
4. The Future – laid to the right of the Significator and Crossing

This spread shows cards symbolizing: the past of the event (its causes); the present circumstances and challenges; and its outcome. This spread may be applied to an event, a decision to be made, or a psychological process which requires thought and action.

When the cards are carefully and completely shuffled, make sure that half the deck is reversed by taking the cards, cutting them and laying them down on the table as two stacks. Turn one of the stacks upside down. The pack which remains upright is your conscious mind, while the reversed pack is your unconscious mind. Shuffle them together to integrate alchemically your conscious and unconscious, and then begin the spread.

A sample interpretation to a question will illustrate the process of stating and understanding the spread.

Question:
What is the significance of my meeting today with John Smith?

The Cards:

PAST

PRESENT
WITH CROSSING

FUTURE

Figure 8   The Past-Present-Future Spread

The Answer:

1. The Significator = Wheel of Fortune (upright)
At the present time you are aware that you are open to taking chances with relationships and exploring your abilities to open up to others, whatever their beliefs. You are inclined to take risks with your ideas and understanding of others, and are therefore likely to be fortunate in this relationship, which will provide you with opportunities to grow.

2. The Crossing = The Lovers (reversed)
You are unlikely to be aware of the implications of the relationship you are initiating with this individual, particularly because

you value the process over the outcome. In accepting whatever relationships come along, you are undervaluing yourself and lessening your self worth. By exerting more discrimination and control, you will create a higher awareness within yourself (and others), rather than be prone to infatuations or brotherly-sisterly communications which are not equal and challenging for you.

3. The Past = The Fool (upright)
You are conscious that in the past you have been enthusiastic and spontaneous in your response to new people in your life, without considering your own needs or understanding the implications of the relationship. You have either accepted them completely or rejected their company, without allowing a negotiation between you. As a result, your ability to make appropriate relationships has been unpredictable and unsure.

4. The Future = The Star (reversed)
Although you may not be aware of it, you are entering a relationship which will force you to take responsibility for yourself, will access deep areas and reverse life-long patterns. You are being led into a process of change which has been experienced by many, and in some ways are responding to collective impulses rather than personal ones. In order to attain fulfilment in this relationship you must be more conscious of who you are and how you relate to others.

Because the first two cards were upright and the last two reversed, the querent would be expected to move from areas in which he/she is conscious to a relationship which is increasingly unconscious, yet taps and utilizes deeper levels of their self-awareness. Such a trend is important to identify, and the movement from the Fool to the Star does follow the natural evolution of tarot itself, from naivety to a recognition of one's own worth through changing life patterns. In this sense the reading may initiate and aid further and deeper understanding of life motives.

This spread is helpful for obtaining feedback about decisions or actions to be undertaken, or for providing directions in navigating through personal, psychological processes.

THE FOUR FUNCTION SPREAD

This spread shows the status of the four psychological functions according to Jung (*Psychological Types*, pp. 517–617), oriented around the significator and crossing in an X-shape.

In order to utilize this spread it would be valuable to define the four functions. *Sensation* simply transmits inner or outer physical stimulus to perception; it is the way you sense the world around and within you. *Intuition* transmits perceptions in an unconscious way as an instinctive apprehension which seems whole and right; it is the way you receive complete conceptions about the world. *Feeling* imparts a definite value to either conscious or unconscious contents; it is your hierarchy of feelings about the world. *Thinking* brings given representations into a conceptual connection with each other through either unintentional or intentional judgement; it is how you think about the world and yourself. Each of these four functions are necessary for a balanced life, and this spread indicates which functions are dominant and which are inferior. It is natural that, due to the pressures of our lives, we develop some functions before others and tend to overdevelop one or two of the functions at the expense of the others. This spread can indicate how to redress the balance.

In the spread, the upper left card is the Thinking Function, the upper right the Feeling Function, the lower left the Sensation Function, and the lower right the Intuition Function. The Thinking and Feeling functions above are called 'rational' in that they are influenced by reflection, while the Sensation and Intuition functions below are called 'irrational' in that they aim at pure perception. In this spread we can see the qualities attached to each of these four functions, and in the centre the course of action for resolution or integration. Reversed cards in this spread indicate inferior qualities attached to certain of the functions, or unconsciousness about their action.

The spread shows the functions in present time, although it can be used for an analysis of past states and in anticipation of future states as well.

The deck should be shuffled and cut, and the significator placed in the centre of the table, with the crossing diagonally placed across it. Next cut the deck into four piles, one for each of the functions. Place one in each of the four directions away from the significator, and turn over the top card of each pile.

A sample reading would appear as follows:

1. Significator (centre) = The Moon reversed
Your integrating principle is feelings, where a set of values are established against which you compare all inner and outer perceptions. However, your values are largely unconscious, that is you are unaware of the criteria which determine your own feelings. In order to achieve the path of integration, you must learn to understand positive and negative feelings and apportion energy to them in a conscious way.

2. Crossing (across the Significator) =
The Emperor reversed
Your primary obstacle is an irrational tendency to impose your will on others, particularly in order to control more unconscious aspects of yourself. You must have more confidence in your creative abilities and realize that your path is correct and will inevitably lead to positive results and increased integration if you allow feelings and affections to rise and be expressed freely.

3. Sensation Function (lower left) = The Chariot reversed
Your sensations are affected by deep emotional difficulties from your past of which you are only gradually becoming aware. Your instincts govern you too much and you need to regain control over your body, and by extension, your environment. Sensation is an inferior function for you now.

4. Intuition Function (lower right) = The Empress
Your intuitions tell you that a harmonious direction will only follow if you are truthful to close partners or associates – they

121

THINKING

FEELING

SENSATION

SIGNIFICATOR (SELF)
AND CROSSING

INTUITION

Figure 9   The Four Function Spread

need to know how you feel, no matter how difficult it may be to tell them. You have a large picture of a creative goal and must learn how to bring that into being while considering those around you. Try to integrate your visions with others.

5. Feeling Function (upper right) = Wheel of Fortune
You take chances with your feelings, and at the moment they are quite random in their actions. You are getting it right most of the time because you are staying open and aware through it all. You can expect positive influences and good feelings for your pains.

6. Thinking Function (upper left) = The Lovers reversed
Thoughts of love and integration are premature and do not take your unconscious wishes into consideration, or you are entering a relationship the true significance of which

is unclear to you. When confronted by choices between outer appearances and inner worth, you still tend to prefer appearances. Controlling your thoughts with meditation or improving your concentration will bring great dividends.

The spread shows that the Sensation and Thinking functions are dominant because·they are upright, and that the Intuition and Feeling functions are inferior or undervalued at the moment. This type of spread shows in which areas of our lives we must look more closely and where within ourselves we must learn to act from the heart.

THE CELTIC CROSS SPREAD

The Celtic Cross is a classic spread, known to have been used since the Middle Ages. Its function is to show a range of possibilities at a given moment, although a more modern way of interpreting the spread is to discover the level of awareness and the conditions acting upon a querent. The spread utilizes the cross shape and also four further cards in a vertical line. We will illustrate both the traditional interpretation of this spread and then its more contemporary form.

The Traditional Celtic Cross Spread

The traditional Celtic Cross spread is often done with major arcana cards only. Therefore separate out the twenty-two major arcana cards and place them in numerical order on the table before the querent. Have the querent shuffle the cards while thinking about the question, and then state the question. Upon stating the question, have the querent place the cards down.

The cards should be placed in the following sequence:

1. **Present Position – in the middle**. Represents the present situation and circumstances of the querent.
2. **Immediate Influences – crosses it**. Shows the domain of the question and the blockages and obstacles to be anticipated.
3. **Destiny – crowns it**. The goals and ultimate destiny of the querent.

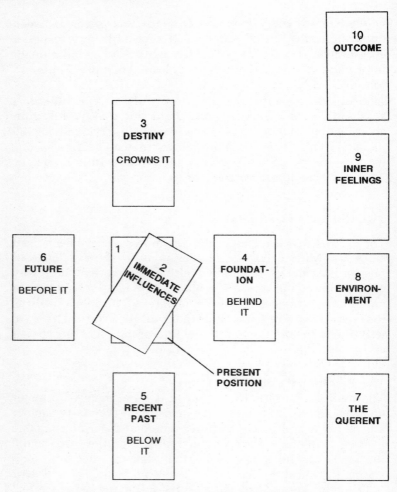

Figure 10   The Traditional Celtic Cross Spread

4. **Foundation – is behind it**. Basic influences which existed in the past as a foundation of the question.
5. **Recent Past – below it**. Influences which are passing or have just passed through the life of the querent.
6. **Future – before it**. Where the question will lead the querent.

Then, in a vertical line beginning at the bottom:

7. **The querent – at the bottom**. Present situation and presenting issues of the querent.
8. **Environment – above it**. The influence of the querent on others and their influence upon the querent.
9. **Inner Feelings – above it**. The hopes, fears and inner feelings as well as secrets of the querent.
10. **Outcome – at the top**. The outcome which results from the previous nine cards.

In the interpretation the reader will discover relationships between cards or positions which allow the querent to make connections which may not be obvious to him/her. Some cards will be particularly interesting to the querent, and not others. This may indicate areas in which the querent would be well advised to study 'his' actions and implications more fully. There may, for example, be a connection between the immediate influences and the recent past. Cards in the spread which are reversed will indicate areas in which the querent is likely to be unaware or unconscious of 'his' actions and need further attention.

The Psychological Celtic Cross Spread

The Celtic Cross can also be used with a more psychological or personal growth orientation. For this spread, we will use the entire deck of cards. The rank of the card occupying each position shows its relative importance. Major arcana cards show archetypal forces or actions; court cards show individuals or subpersonalities of the querent who affect the issue; and minor arcana cards show events through which developments occur. Reversed cards show areas of unconsciousness and also identify blockages or obstructions which will require additional attention and penetration.

Shuffle the cards and cut them into two piles, placing them next to each other. The lefthand cards refer to the dynamics of the present situation and the righthand cards refer to the four vertical cards which describe the elements or psychological functions. From the lefthand deck place a Significator, a Crossing over it, Conscious Mind above it, Unconscious Mind below it, the Past to the left of it, and the Future to the right of it. From the righthand deck place four cards from bottom to top to the right of the cross, and call them Physical on the bottom, Emotional second up, Mental third up and Spiritual at the top.

The sequence of cards is as follows:

1. **Significator**. The querent; the question; the central issue; potential growth; the principle of integration and synthesis; the self; self-knowledge; the centre of consciousness.

2. **Crossing over it**. Obstructions; conditions preventing growth; barriers to understanding; restrictions, whether imposed by others or the self; masks; delusions or illusions; the bridge across which resolution acts; boundaries which require penetration; self-betrayal.

3. **Conscious Mind above it**. Objectivity; conscious attitudes and goals; realizations; spiritual aspirations; individualization; self-confidence.

4. **Unconscious Mind below it**. Subjectivity; unconscious issues, instincts and urges; hopes; obscurity of self; feelings; family attitudes; the desire to merge with others; lack of self-confidence through unconsciousness.

5. **The Past to the left, behind it**. The past; the environment and its influences; earlier opportunities and obstacles; the birth of a development; self-confidence; self-assertion.

6. **The Future to the right, ahead of it**. The future; partners, associates and relationships; the outside world; reliance on others; ability to relate and delegate; assuming responsibility; sublimation of the self.

7. **Physical World at the bottom right**. External reality; the body; finances; health and well-being; the quality of action; creativity; groundedness; security; decision-making abilities.

8. **Emotional World above it**. Inner reality; feelings; dreamlife and unconscious reality; emotional responses and reactions; value systems; relationships; needs and wants; friends and family circumstances.

9. **Mental World above it**. Mentality; identification with self and others; governing ideas; concepts; beliefs; the

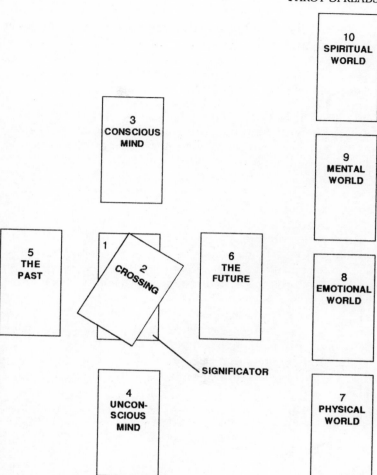

Figure 11   *The Psychological Celtic Cross Spread*

capacity to communicate, listen and understand; attitudes; thoughts and the thinking process; hopes and fears.

10. **Spiritual World at the top**. Spirituality; intuition; visionary reality; perception, especially higher perception; energy; purity; higher goals and aspirations; expressions of release; disidentification.

This spread is interpreted as you have seen in the other examples.

THE ASTROLOGICAL SPREAD

This spread is called the Astrological Spread because it utilizes twelve cards around the significator which correspond to the signs or houses of astrology (see Figure 12). The starting point of this spread is the card to the left, the Ascendant, where the sun rises in the morning in the east. From the Ascendant you proceed in a counter-clockwise direction around the circle.

The great virtue of this spread is that you can apply it to virtually any time period and therefore interpret a process which will take place or has taken place. Each card around the circle can signify a period of time. If each card represents one month, the spread can describe one year of twelve months. It can also describe twelve hours, twenty-four hours (two hours each), twelve days, twelve weeks, two years (two months each), etc. It is obviously easier if the time period is divisible by twelve, although any time period could be used.

The implication is that the spread shows a development of the question or individual through a particular time period. The spread can be used as feedback for the process of psychological or spiritual development, as a predictive tool, or as a matrix for answering particular concerns of the querent.

The Astrological Spread can be done with either the Four Function Spread or the first six cards of the Celtic Cross Spread within its centre, allowing the combination of a time period with general concerns about one's psychological or spiritual orientation within it. The positions in the Astrological Spread are as follows:

1st House – Ascendant – Aries. The personality and its issues; physical appearances; self-assertion; the ability to bond with self or others.
2nd House – Taurus. Self-valuation; acceptance of the tangible world; physical reality and the body; money and possessions.

3rd House – Gemini. Communication; the instinctive and unconscious mind; initial education; self-expression and variety; flexibility; short journeys; relationships with brothers and sisters.

4th House – Cancer. The family system and environment; parents and their emotional values; early environment; wants and needs; feelings of kinship and belonging; identity and roots.

5th House – Leo. Exteriorizing the self; primary education; relationships with teachers; games and gameplaying; acting; the arts, leisure and sport; consciousness of self.

6th House – Virgo. Practical service; the health; puberty and early relationships; discrimination and distillation of experience; work attitudes and relations; making life choices.

7th House – Libra. Relationships; sublimating the self in others or the world; needs and functions of relationships; emotional, business and marital relationships; relations with the world; diplomacy.

8th House – Scorpio. The process of life and death; sexuality and conception; the metaphysical; reincarnation and past lives; others' money, feelings, ideas and energies; business affairs; magic.

9th House – Sagittarius. Religion, psychology and philosophy of life; higher union and mind; beliefs; foreign journeys; legal matters and the law; athletics.

10th House – Capricorn. Ego consciousness; identification with goals and objectives in life; higher aspirations; career and occupation; parents; selfishness; pragmatism and practicality.

11th House – Aquarius. Selfless love; integration with groups or organizations; New Age concepts; sense of community; creativity and communication of ideas; social ambitions and aims; politics.

12th House – Pisces. Dissolution and inner perception; isolation and loneliness; spiritual service and sacrifice; seclusion and privacy; institutions and large organizations; secrets.

In using the Astrological Spread it is possible to selectively use certain houses/signs which refer to specific questions or issues raised, or to describe an entire sequence of influences.

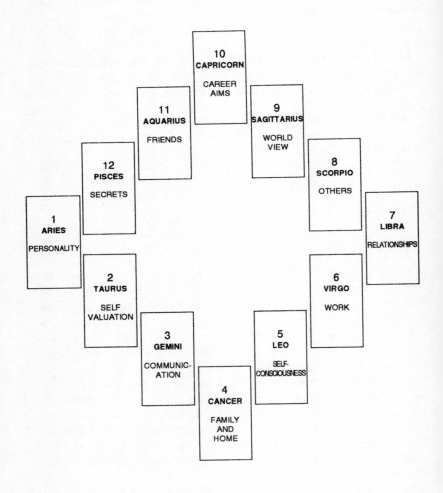

Figure 12 The Astrological Spread

Once again, the major arcana cards will identify areas of primary importance and archetypal activity; the court cards will show particular individuals who will affect or bring certain personality issues to the fore; and the minor arcana cards will describe more mundane events which happen in specific areas or at certain times. The combination of cards yields a rich tapestry which can be interpreted psychologically or as a fund of information.

PSYCHOSYNTHESIS SPREAD

One example is an adaptation of a known psychological model, such as Roberto Assagioli's Egg Diagram of Our Psyche (See Ferrucci, *What We May Be*, p.44). Assagioli defines seven levels of being located on the Egg Diagram, each of which represent an aspect of the self in its process of achieving transpersonal being. The cards may be laid out as shown in Figure 13.

The cards are laid down in the following sequence:

1. Lower Unconscious: the beginner in us; personal psychological past; repressed complexes and forgotten memories of importance.
2. Middle Unconscious: skills and mental states which can be willed into action.
3. Superconscious: our evolutionary future states and expressions of knowing, being and feeling.
4. Field of Consciousness: the field of action, environment and present circumstances; current ideas and attitudes, feelings and intuitions.
5. Personal self or 'I': sense of identity and identification; level of awareness.
6. Transpersonal Self: the principle of individuation; centredness and identity with higher being; being-consciousness or bliss and the will to achieve it.
7. Collective Unconscious: our attitude to the preconditions of our lives; the matrix from which we arose and within which we live; the field of combat or integration of the self.

131

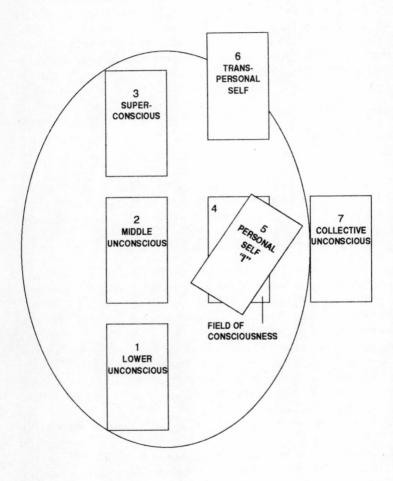

Figure 13   The Psychosynthesis Spread

When tarot is used in this way it becomes a valuable psychotherapeutic tool which can be used by therapists or individuals wishing to expand their awareness of self.

INVENT YOUR OWN SPREAD

The spreads shown above demonstrate the basic principles of tarot, but it will, I hope, be clear that the cards may be used in other original and unique ways also. You can construct any set of values about which you wish feedback and utilize the tarot to discover clues or images which will aid you in the process of self-discovery.

THE MAGICIAN.

8 · TAROT AND SELF-DEVELOPMENT

The principles which guide this book lie within the domain of self-development and transpersonal psychology as they are contained within and overlap into tarot. What follows are some aids to the process of learning and using the tarot which compare with the process encountered when discovering, affirming, persisting with and directly experiencing the self within.

Our view of the tarot starts with the idea of the self, of the individual, and our experiences of identity with that self. While the tarot cards picture kings, queens, magicians, maidens and knights, all the images are symbolic of the self and represent stages of its process of coming into being. We are constantly developing our individuality, and making our potentials actual.

The actions depicted in the cards are parts of our own process crystallized in symbols. We are looking to align ourselves with a meaning in our lives, and the interpretation of the cards may shed light on the deeper mechanisms our quest embodies. We must learn to value each part of ourselves and all those around us, as well as understand our inner needs and aspirations, so that we may determine and maintain the correct priorities. The tarot cards may point us towards areas we over- or undervalue in our lives.

We are always confronted with the need to take responsibility for the decisions which form our life, and to understand the overt and hidden motivations which lead us to take certain choices. Often these critical events are passed by choosing the path of least resistance, but we must realize the implications of such choices and learn to be more conscious about them.

The life process is difficult at best, but nonetheless we must learn to balance its inherent seriousness against the need to play, to enjoy ourselves, our relationships and the world around us. The importance of learning when to concentrate and when to relax and forget, when to burrow into crisis and when to detach from outer events − all these phases and rhythms of life must be understood as being integral parts of the whole. Tarot is capable of giving us some indication of these rhythms, their nature and their timings.

We all look to the future, both with positive expectations and also a sense of dread. Our anticipation and the way in which we approach the future is a primary factor in the way we live our lives, and understanding it involves experimenting with the many possible futures we each carry. Thus it is that the divinatory capabilities of the tarot interact with its psychotherapeutic qualities to create dynamic visions of our future.

At the last, we are all very different individuals, with needs and expectations unique to each of us. While we may seek friendship and evaluation from our family, friends and counsellors, the ultimate responsibility for our lives rests with us. We must therefore accept the great diversity of viewpoints we carry, and work and play with our journey in our own unique way. It is important to not only study tarot, but to learn it, make it a tool for your own understanding of yourself, and become your own guide in the process of being.

Our thoughts define us to an extent that we rarely recognize. When we are in a bad mood our entire life and its directions seem invalid, but when we are positive and creative our life seems extremely pleasant and we look forward to each new day. Experimentation shows that we can modify and support our mental definition of ourselves in three similar ways: meditation, creative visualization and affirmation.

MEDITATION

Meditation has many forms, including prayer, bringing the conscious mind under control, relaxation, spiritual exercises, consciousness-raising, and the systematic investigation of a particular idea. The most common techniques involve using a key such as a mantra which is repeatedly spoken, counting and visualizing breaths, or using an image or mandala as a focus for the mind.

The tarot cards are perfectly suited as subjects for meditation because they contain imagery which supports the archetypes that you may wish to explore. By spending a period of time looking at a particular card, soaking up its details, feeling the intensity of the colours, seeing the interactions of the shapes, trying to understand and respond to the ideas behind the images, we can bring these same qualities into our own life. At times when we are depressed or lack direction it can be very helpful to meditate on a card which has the strength or direction we lack.

It is natural while meditating to be tempted to go off the track, to see and feel things which are beyond the card you are using as an embarkation point. When this happens, recognize what it is that brings you off centre, how it makes you feel, identify where it comes from, and bring your mind back to the original subject. By maintaining concentration we are eventually able to identify more and more deeply with the intention of the card.

The ability to meditate upon the tarot cards can bring your mind under control and utilize its further capabilities which will benefit you in your daily life. The cards can support, reinforce and amplify all of the qualities you wish to express in your life. When you need energy and dominance, meditate on the Emperor. When you feel reflective and open to dreams and fantasies about your future, meditate on the Moon.

As an exercise, meditate on one card of the tarot each day for ten minutes. Reflect on the qualities that the card possesses, and also upon the feelings, thoughts, spiritual insights and sensations that accompany your meditation. They will provide you with clues which will lead to further development of your self. When you reach a point where you feel the content is either uninteresting or you get bored with the imagery, that is a signal that you are coming into contact with deeper levels of your own being and should proceed beyond and push through your resistances. Insights into your life and your self often come at the point when you are experiencing the greatest resistance.

Familiarity with the tarot cards will tap you into a deep stream of knowledge and understanding which you will find refreshing and stimulating. After some time you will begin to understand the higher implications of the images, the transpersonal levels which lie beyond your normal state.

CREATIVE VISUALIZATION

Our being operates simultaneously at four levels, indicated by the psychological functions of sensation, feeling, thinking and intuition, as we have seen (see p.72). We are continually experimenting, redefining, rerunning and anticipating the events of our lives in our minds. The precision or vagueness of our imagination can have an influence upon our ability to bring our desired reality into being. Imagination is a valuable tool which we should take maximum advantage of because it is one of the most creative and important functions of the psyche.

The psychologist Roberto Assagioli created psychosynthesis as a series of techniques to develop the self and to gain access to transpersonal levels of awareness, and utilized visualization extensively in his exercises. He accepted as a fundamental fact that images have equivalent emotional and physical components which correspond to them. (See his *Psychosynthesis*, p. 145.) Images have great power and can change our lives.

Visualization helps concentration and also provides a way for us to influence our will, our ability to bring our self to awareness. If we have a friend quietly speak the guided

137

imagery for one of the tarot cards while we are relaxed and with our eyes closed, we can enter into the experience of the tarot, feel its colours, imagine its landscapes, bring the qualities carried by the card into our lives in a real way. We can allow our self to enter into the world of the card, to surrender to its environment and its atmosphere.

With practice it becomes easier and easier to be receptive to the images of the cards, to let them dwell in our minds, and even to reflect upon them when we are not looking at them. Through time we learn to identify with the cards, with the archetypal states they represent, and therefore bring our natural intuition to the fore and stimulate our basic creativity.

When we visualize climbing up a steep mountain, it supports our abilities to ascend in consciousness. To dive down into a deep pool of water reinforces our ability to penetrate our deepest feelings and bring back their valuable contents. When we walk through a bright and summery meadow in our visualization, we feel the warmth, and feel better psychologically. By using the cards in this way it is possible to extend your range of feelings, ideas and spiritual perceptions dramatically.

AFFIRMATIONS

Once we have identified the qualities of one of the major arcana cards that we wish to more actively bring into our life, we can use the affirmation associated with the card. The use of an affirmation can go beyond simply willing a change to come into being. The affirmation is an active matrix of commands made to our inner self, repeated regularly, and reinforced repeatedly. The strength of the affirmation, its language and its concepts, will determine how powerful its effect upon you will be.

The potency of an affirmation depends upon how seriously you take it. It must become an article of your faith that the principle expressed is valuable, indeed essential for you to have in your life. It is an adventure, but one which you can benefit from if you are able to bring your will into line with the potency of the affirmation. Like using creative visualization with tarot, you may experience resistance or a kind of backlash from your affirmation, but this often is a signal that the affirmation and its underlying energy is being taken in.

THE MAGICIAN.

9 · TAKING TAROT FURTHER

Probably the most valuable way to increase your understanding and familiarity with the tarot is to keep a dedicated psychological workbook for use with the tarot. It has been shown in modern psychotherapy that keeping a workbook or diary to monitor your progress is a primary and important way to record the workings of your inner life, your unfolding awareness of who you are, and a guide to the way in which your journey develops.

The primary concern of the workbook should be the development of your inner life. It is a good idea to write down any dreams or fantasies you have about yourself, to draw or sketch any symbols that evoke feelings in you, whether or not you understand them. The workbook is an important document because it is your way of keeping in touch with your inner process.

There are many reasons for keeping such a workbook, but the most important is to learn to formulate your inner realities for the benefit of your conscious mind. The clearer and more precisely you describe your process, the more satisfied you will be with your progress. While writing, you will need constantly to go back to the cards to see what they actually show or mean. You tend to remember what you want to, not what is there. You will see the ambiguities in your descriptions easily, and will learn with each new view to resolve them in a more fluid manner.

When you have difficult times, or harbour aggressive or violent feelings, feelings of sadness or disgust, you can give them full vent by writing about them in the workbook. The images which evoke your inner being will be significant to you for the rest of your life, and it is essential to become familiar with their sources and their mechanisms. You will see that certain symbols recur again and again – they must be telling you something important about your deeper self.

The cards you draw are like the people for whom you do readings – they evoke your inner processes and allow them an avenue to the surface so that they can become a familiar part of your whole rather than an episode which pops up when you least expect it. You will see the resonance between your outer life and inner development, and whether the two are in harmony or out of balance. Tarot pictures your attitude to yourself, and using it as a friend and guide will indicate whether your balancing mechanism, the psyche, is being fully used.

Expand your vocabulary of cards until you know all seventy-eight of them. Experiment with other decks which explore different symbol systems, such as goddess tarots or astrological tarots or other antique decks. You will find that the broader your interests in these ideas, the more fully engaged in the world of the psyche you are. Tarot is truly a guide to enlightenment.

THE MAGICIAN

GLOSSARY

Aether – The quintessence, the fifth element, an invisible force which unifies the other four elements.

Affirmation – A statement or declaration repeatedly made to oneself as a way of training the will.

Arcana – Secret, mysterious or hidden knowledge.

Archetype – The representation or symbol of an energy principle which has been in existence within the human psyche at all times and in all cultures.

Archetypal world – The domain of the archetypes.

Brotherhood of the Rosy Cross – A mystical order, similar to the Masons, which originated in the seventeenth century; also called the Rosicrucians.

Cabbala – The mystical teaching of Judaism which has the diagram known as the Tree of Life as one of its central aspects.

Caduceus – A wand with two snakes entwining it, surmounted by wings or a winged helmet, which symbolizes energy, healing force or the integration of lower and higher being.

Cardinal – An astrological term meaning the initiatory or activating principles and houses.

Cartomancy – Telling fortunes with tarot or other cards.

Chakras – Energy centres within the body which govern and modulate physical, mental and spiritual being.

Collective unconscious – A level of consciousness beyond the personal unconscious in which the past common experiences and the acquired wisdom of the human species is stored.

Conscious – The part of our psyche which is concerned with adjustment to external reality.

Decanates – Ten degree segments of the astrological signs.

Dis-identification – Consciously releasing one's identification with a particular way of being or subpersonality in order to step outside and observe it.

Divination – The process of arriving at the answer to a question by interpreting symbolic patterns created naturally or by one's own actions, such as with the tarot.

Ego – The vehicle of our own personal goals and objectives in life, which lies at the centre of the field of consciousness.

Esoteric – Inner teaching only available to initiates.

Exoteric – Outer teaching available to everyone.

Fixed – An astrological term signifying sustaining or unchangeable principles or houses.

Four worlds – The planes of existence according to the cabbalists: the Archetypal World, the World of Creation, the World of Formation, and the World of Action.

Gematria – A mystical system of correlations of numbers with the letters of the Hebrew or Greek alphabet.

Golden section proportion – A geometric ratio in which two parts have the same relationship as the larger part to the whole, found in natural growth processes.

Guided imagery – A sequence of images which are followed using the imagination with the intention of activating the will towards a particular goal.

Hermetic – A body of mystical literature celebrating the mysteries of the Greek god Hermes.

Individuation – A gradual process of understanding and bringing into balance the different components of the psyche and thereby making the person whole.

Immum Coeli – Latin for 'bottom of the heavens', the lowest and most unconscious position in an astrological horoscope.

Karma – Our attachment to previous patterns of being and action in this and previous lives.

Magic – The act of utilizing the will to achieve an end.

Magical weapons – The sword, wand, pentacle and cup are instruments symbolizing the forces of mind, energy, matter and feelings available to the magician.

Mandala – A circular meditation diagram expressing the principle of wholeness.

Mantic art – An art of divination.

Mantra – Spoken or hummed syllables which are the secret seed or essence of a divinity; used in Eastern religious practices to concentrate the mind and join with the godhead.

Meditation – A technique for stilling the mind, for achieving focus or concentration, often using breathing, sounds or images as a basis.

Mutable – An astrological term signifying movable or changeable principles or houses.

Myth – Stories of goddesses, gods, heroines and heros which illustrate archetypal principles.

Numerology – A system of attributing qualities to the sequence of numbers.

Order of the Golden Dawn – A mystic order founded in the nineteenth century in which A.E. Waite and Aleister Crowley were initiates.

Planetary spheres – The ancients visualized planetary spheres surrounding Earth, each ring containing gods and goddesses. Ascending through the spheres meant moving from lower lunar unconsciousness to higher levels of godlike being.

Pillar – One of the three vertical columns of sephira in the tree of life, either positive, negative or neutral in charge.

Psyche – All psychological processes, both conscious and unconscious, including the soul and mind, the centre of which is the ego.

Psychosynthesis – A system of techniques to evoke and facilitate psychological integration.

Querent – An individual asking a question or consulting the oracle.

Rosicrucian – A Renaissance mystical Order of the Rose Cross founded by Christian Rosencreutz.

Rota – Latin for wheel, and an anagram of taro.

Sephiroth (pl. sephira) – Emanations from the divine which manifest in the four worlds as phases of evolution or consciousness, or steps through which the soul unfolds its realization of the cosmos.

Shadow – Undeveloped or unconscious aspects of our personality which we tend to hide, repress or project onto others.

Subpersonality – One of the many possible components of the total personality, each of which acts in its own way.

Suit – In tarot the suits pentacles, wands, cups and swords are related to a magical weapon, element or psychological function.

Symbol – A manifestation of an archetypal pattern which carries multiple meanings.

Synchronicity – A connecting principle of events, feelings, or states of mind, which goes beyond cause and effect, and functions through meaningful coincidence.

Thoth – The Egyptian god of writing.

Torah – The Hebrew book of the law.

Transpersonal – The universal core of being which lies beyond the personal realm.

Tree of Life – A mystical diagram showing the unfolding or manifestation of the universe through ten sephiroth (spheres or levels of being) connected by twenty-two paths (channels of divine influence).

Trumps – Derived from the Latin *trionfi*, a circular procession, but now the superior cards.

Unconscious – All thoughts and feelings, both personal and collective, of which we are not conscious.

Western Mystery Tradition – A traditional system of hidden knowledge passed on in the west and originating from Egypt and Greece.

Will – The psychological function which tends to bring the personality in line with the purposes of the higher self.

Yin-yang – A Chinese symbol of spiralling masculine and feminine forces.

THE MAGICIAN.

BIBLIOGRAPHY

Anonymous, *Meditations on the Tarot*, Element, Shaftesbury, 1991.

Arrien, Angeles, *The Tarot Handbook*, Aquarian Press, London, 1991.

Assagioli, Roberto, *Psychosynthesis*, Crucible, London, 1990.

Blakeley, John, *The Mystical Tower of the Tarot*, Watkins, London, 1974.

Butler, Bill, *Dictionary of the Tarot*, Schocken Books, New York, 1978.

Campbell, Joseph & Roberts, Richard, *Tarot Revelations*, Vernal Equinox, San Anselmo, 1979.

Camphausen, Rufus, *Mind Mirror and Tree-of-Life Tarot Cards*, privately published, Amsterdam, 1981.

Cavendish, Richard, *The Tarot*, Chancellor Press, London, 1975.

Circlot, J. E., *A Dictionary of Symbols*, Routledge, London, 1988.

Count Goblet d'Alviella, *The Migration of Symbols*, Aquarian Press, Wellingborough, 1979 (1892).

Crowley, Aleister, *The Book of Thoth (Egyptian Tarot)*, Samuel Weiser, York Beach, 1975 (1944).

Ferrucci, Piero, *What We May Be*, Turnstone Press, London, 1982.

Fortune, Dion, *The Mystical Qabalah*, Ernest Benn, London, 1974.

Greene, Liz and Sharman-Burke, Juliet, *The Mythic Tarot*, Rider, London, 1986.

Haich, Elisabeth, *The Wisdom of Tarot*, Allen & Unwin, London, 1985.

Hoeller, Stephen, *The Royal Road*, Quest Books, Wheaton, 1975.

Jacobi, Dr Jolande, *The Psychology of C. G. Jung*, Kegan Paul, London, 1942.

James, Laura DeWitt, *William Blake and the Tree of Life*, Shambhala, Berkeley, 1971.

Jung, Carl G., *Psychological Types*, Kegan Paul Trench Trubner, London, 1923.

Kaplan, Stuart R., *The Classical Tarot*, Aquarian Press, Wellingborough, 1972.

. . ., *The Encyclopedia of Tarot*, U.S. Games Systems, New York, 1978.

Knight, Gareth, *A Practical Guide to Qabalistic Symbolism, Volume Two*, Kahn & Averill, London, 1986.

. . ., *The Treasure House of Images*, Aquarian, Wellingborough, 1986.

Mann, A. T., *The Mandala Astrological Tarot*, Macmillan, London, 1987.

Nichols, Sallie, *Jung and Tarot*, Weiser, New York, 1980.

Ouspensky, P. D., *A New Model of the Universe*, Kegan Paul, London, 1931.

Smith, Caroline and Astrop, John, *Elemental Tarot*, Dolphin Doubleday, London, 1988.

Tilley, Roger, *Playing Cards*, Weidenfeld and Nicholson, London, 1967.

Waite, Arthur Edward, *The Pictorial Key to the Tarot*, Rider & Company, London, 1974 (1910).

Walker, Barbara G., *The Secrets of the Tarot*, Harper & Row, San Francisco, 1984.

Whitmore, Diana, *Psychosynthesis Counselling in Action*, Sage, London, 1991.

Williams, Charles, *The Greater Trumps*, Sphere, London, 1975 (1932).

THE MAGICIAN.

INDEX